07-CPX-012

D0122694

Trusteeship in the Private College

TRUSTEESHIP IN THE PRIVATE COLLEGE

Miriam Mason Wood

THE JOHNS HOPKINS UNIVERSITY PRESS
Baltimore and London

Parts of this text have appeared previously in two journal articles. Acknowledgment is made to the American Council on Education and Educational Record *for Miriam M. Wood, "Crosscurrents and Undercurrents in the Trustee-President Relationship,"* Educational Record *65 (Winter 1984) and to the* Harvard Business Review *for Miriam M. Wood, "What Role for College Trustees?"* Harvard Business Review *(May–June 1983), Copyright 1983 by the President and Fellows of Harvard College, all rights reserved.*

The Johns Hopkins University Press, 701 West 40th Street,
Baltimore, Maryland 21211
The Johns Hopkins Press Ltd., London

The paper in this book is acid-free and meets the guidelines for permanence and durability of the Committee on Production Guidelines for Book Longevity of the Council on Library Resources.

Library of Congress Cataloging-in-Publication Data

Wood, Miriam Mason.
  Trusteeship in the private college.

  Revision of the author's Ph.D. thesis—Harvard University, 1982, originally published under title: The board of trustees of the private liberal arts college.
  Bibliography: p.
  Includes index.
  1. College trustees. I. Wood, Miriam Mason. Board of Trustees of the private liberal arts college.
II. Title.
LB2341.W575   1985   378′.1011   85-8051
ISBN 0-8018-3270-5 (alk. paper)

To C.O.W. III

Contents

Foreword
by David Riesman

In the United States there are fewer than two hundred nonsectarian liberal arts colleges with student bodies under twenty-five hundred. At their frequent best, this genre of institution has been a national resource. Those whose names we know—Pomona, Reed, Colorado, Whitman; Sweet Briar, Hollins; Carleton, Grinnell, Oberlin; and then a number of colleges of high selectivity and intellectual vivacity in New England and the Mid-Atlantic states—illustrate the possibility of combining the role of dedicated teacher and nonreclusive scholar. This whole group of colleges has prepared a disproportionately large number of the intellectual, academic, corporate, professional, and governmental leaders of this country, both men and women. The outstanding women's colleges among them (to my dismay a somewhat endangered species as more and more men's and women's colleges have become coeducational) continue to prepare women with the self-confidence to enter such fields as physics and engineering, previously dominated in the United States as a matter of course by men. The life of a professor looks inviting to many undergraduates in a liberal arts college, in contrast to the undergraduates in the liberal arts college of a research university, who may meet as many harried as invitational graduate students and junior faculty. Many colleges in this genre of institution have had a modest success in providing noncondescending support to their minority students.

While the day-to-day affairs of these colleges are in the hands primarily of their faculty members and to a lesser extent of their administration, it is of course their trustees who bear the responsibility for the long-term future. It is the trustees who make the final decision in selecting a president and at whose pleasure the president then serves; it is the trustees who safeguard and, in the best cases, increase the endowment; it is the trustees who support the president, where the buck usually stops, and who can buffer the institution against outside interference, whether from the local community, inflamed alumni, or state and national government. The trustees are the ultimate goalies.

The college trustee is an American invention. The role of trustee in the independent sector is also an illustration of the sorts of volunteer energy that so struck Tocqueville when he visited the United States in 1831. College trustees are unpaid, though some lawyers and perhaps others may indirectly profit from useful contacts. But on the maxim that one goes to the busiest person to get something done, the most influential trustees are quite commonly those for whom the work is not in the service of their already eminent careers but in the service of the institution and, with varying degrees of camaraderie, of their fellow board members. However, because the work is unpaid, presidents and board officers who would like members to be more active have no sanctions to employ against those who may show up at a football game or commencement but who do not serve on the more arduous board committees such as the committee on academic affairs or a committee planning a capital campaign, let alone the almost incessant and often stressful work of a search committee for a new president. And since many of the boards studied in Miriam Wood's research are large, with thirty or more members, there is an almost inevitable dilution of responsibility.

Miriam Wood knew before beginning the research reported in this book how important trustees can be. She had herself been a trustee of a business corporation and also of Wilson College, a small and determinedly surviving college for women where she had formerly been an administrator. After a court row concerning decisions by the trustees, she left the College's board. She entered the Harvard Graduate School of Education and made trusteeship the object of her doctoral research. In the crescent literature on trusteeship, Miriam Wood found sage counsel to trustees in books such as the admirable vade mecum by John W. Nason as well as other publications of the increasingly influential Association of Governing Boards of Universities and Colleges. Much has been said concerning the composition of boards of trustees in general, but knowledge is scantier concerning individual boards as they operate at present. Such concreteness is rarely captured in the retrospective histories that have been written concerning a number of the colleges in Miriam Wood's admirably delimited panorama.

Miriam Wood chose a mode of work adapted both to the topic and to her particular talents: case studies of ten liberal arts colleges, all of them in some degree selective and some of them among the most eminent in the nation. She wanted to get beneath the platitudes concerning trustees' responsibilities and hazards. By choosing small colleges, she selected those whose manageable scale permits trustees to become involved—if they are invited in or if they push in—with the details of academic and extracurricular administration. She chose institutions not on the border of solvency but that can be expected to remain afloat and viable for the foreseeable future. That is, she was not in search of basket cases.

Moreover, the scale was equally manageable on her visits to each of the colleges and to the locales where selected trustees, always including the chairman of the board, could talk with her. She gained entrée through the president and made contact then with the chairman of the board and with three additional salient trustees. She promised discretion; those who spoke with her, often extensively and candidly, found the conversation rewarding for their own grasp of the problems they faced vis-à-vis the institution, its leadership, and each other. The book is studded with telling quotations from anguished presidents, troubled trustees, discerning ones, and at times complacent ones. As a trustee, I would find it comforting to discover that issues I was encountering had their parallels elsewhere and illuminating to explore the concrete conflicts and dilemmas board membership can entail. One of the more striking conclusions is how little members of boards of trustees know about one another's views. This is certainly so outside the orbit of the executive committee and indeed in some cases beyond a strong chairman of the particular board or one or two formidable old-timers on the board. Correspondingly, trustees can have very different senses concerning how the president is performing and what, if anything, should be done about it. They meet too seldom to come to know each other well. One of the most useful recommendations the book makes is that the president and the trustees should arrange for occasions when they meet without a formal agenda, to explore ideas about higher education insofar as these might have an influence on the direction of the particular college, perhaps to listen to a speaker from the college or elsewhere—an occasion for intellectual nourishment in addition to the regulation busy-ness. Of course, some trustees enjoy association with a college, and one of the problems some of the presidents in Miriam Wood's study faced is how to cope with trustees who live near the college and for whom it has become a form of occupational therapy.

To be sure, in the best cases the chairman of a board of trustees who works closely with a president can provide an enviable interlocutor, supportive of the president and of the presidential family, and a lucid interpreter of the president and the institution to the less assiduous members of the board. But for most of the time, the board is aware that it is subject to the charge of being a "rubber stamp" for what the president does, just as the president is often a "rubber stamp" for what the faculty decides or, quite as often, refuses consensually to decide. Since the board must ratify, its "rubber stamp," not being automatic, may in fact create anticipatory adherence to presumed board attitudes further down the line in the institution. Yet it is important that the board, along with the president, protect the institution, for example, against too lax and unjustified promotions to tenure or maintaining insufficient reserves against contingencies that might befall enrollments, people, or buildings. However, there are some board members who take their pleasure in their power over the president. In one of the cases studied by the author, an influential board member succeeded in ousting a president in the middle of an academic year.

Most trustees, as this book suggests, find no pleasure but only misery in the thought of dismissing a president whom they have come to know personally, when they have formed any personal ties with him (all ten presidents were male). The prospect of an interregnum is itself an occasion for anxiety, and when a search for a new president is undertaken, all the previously hidden institutional pathologies are likely to erupt; during this period, the actively involved trustees are anything but "rubber stamps." Understandably, there is a loss of effectiveness when a president is on his or her way in or out of office, but it does not follow that the board of trustees gains what the president loses: board-president relations are much too closely inter-linked to be a zero-sum game or, though people play at it, a game at all.

Many boards have a subcommittee whose task it is to consider and nominate prospective members of the board. Sometimes there will be examination, stimulated by such a committee or by an individual, of whether the board is adequate to its task, including the wish to represent newer constituencies, particularly women and blacks and also young alumni and students. Miriam Wood's work is useful in considering the composition of boards. Some board members are helpful because they are professional trustees in the sense of having other responsibilities, and therefore they are not provincial about the particular college board on which they serve. But in other cases it helps to have trustees who are not distracted by competing volunteer activities. *Trusteeship in the Private College* should help alert board members concerning ways to increase their own range and awareness of events in higher education and in the society that would make them better trustees.

Most presidents are not in office long enough to reconstitute a board. To do so they must usually win the confidence of the board and that takes time; board turnover is slow. Their own turnover as presidents may be much faster. What they may be able to do is to shift, though it is delicate, the board chairmanship and key members of the executive committee and thus tilt the board long before it can be seriously reconstituted.

Many of the board members who turn up in Miriam Wood's book are lawyers with Ivy League degrees, members of leading firms. Their time is more flexible than that of many CEOs and lesser officials in corporations and finance. Their legal training gives them a kind of self-confidence that is also found in other successful men and women, including some self-made superconfident ones. Lawyers are perhaps less awed by academics than all but the most superconfident corporate and women volunteer trustees. A lawyer is apt to say, "I know a good man when I see one," as many have said to me in connection with searches and other affairs. Their judgment does not necessarily get better or even more skeptical with time. But the ablest can be very alert and astute; even so, the best of us can be deceived.

Miriam Wood would like to see boards of these private colleges become more representative of the general population, that is, to have more white women members and more than an occasional token black member. Those women members now being added to boards are likely to be women with professional and business careers, sometimes alumnae, in contrast to the more traditional women volunteers whose now frequently deprecated unpaid careers lay in the expertise they developed as volunteers. These paid-career women, like some of the people brought onto the board because they are young and/or black, are sometimes invited to join a good many boards similarly eager to become more representative as well as to provide the new ideas sometimes too generously attributed to new constituencies. A board can run the risk of diluting its own conscientiousness by bringing on members who see themselves as tokens who must give voice to opposition or be regarded as co-opted, and who have not yet been socialized into the responsibilities as well as the platforms that accompany trusteeship.

Dr. Wood shares the widespread and virtually unquestioned assumption that it is a good idea to get the relatively inactive trustees more involved, not to have them simply along for the ride. To mobilize inactive trustees seems as useful a task as the efforts to get nonvoters to the polls, to turn them into active citizens. But I am skeptical of efforts to mobilize the uninvolved, who are also generally the uninformed, because I am aware of the hazards of replacing the judgment of the experienced and committed by the sometimes allergic reactions of the previously somnolent. With trustees as with canines, there is something to the old adage of letting sleeping dogs lie. Yet my own skepticism is chastened by the realization that some episode in the life of the institution, some media event, perhaps some agitated litigant, will arouse the previously unaware trustees in ways that cannot be anticipated, then to swing their newfound weight around; so it may be better to keep them involved at a relatively back-of-the-stove level if one wants to avoid some precipitate action in a crisis.

Is it accidental that several women trustees are quoted who react negatively to the monopoly of board time spent on maintenance and budget and fiscal plans? One asks, "Well, what about the next decade? What direction should the college be going in? Are we prepared to give up liberal arts and start vocational courses? What do we mean by liberal arts?" Another concludes, "It's hard to keep time for both maintenance and looking ahead, thinking ahead." One reflective president remarked to the author that he gains a sense of how trustees view him by the way they are sitting when he comes into the room: "You have to read that silent language." In the author's work it is clear that a board is in trouble when it is vaguely dissatisfied, thinking the president is coasting and not leading yet is not sure if the president can change because so much is a question of nuance, of imperceptible shifts, especially in these colleges where the most selective of them are firmly under faculty control. But the author shows how in this very same situation of cautious and uneasy acquiescence by the board, a trustee cabal may form which may even lead to a president's ouster—less intemperate board members who have slight dissatisfactions with the president, who may have been the second choice or the third choice of the search committee or of the trustees on that committee, may go along with such a coup, perhaps fearing that otherwise, as in one of the colleges discussed at length, matters may drift on for years in uncomfortable but unspecific dissatisfaction. Perhaps only one's spouse or one's closest friend—or a psychotherapist—can at the same time support someone while being critical in ways that might change that person. Miriam Wood quotes one president who says, "I would never appoint a single man to be a president. You can't afford any special social friends [in the campus community]; a professional confidant is possible, but it's not healthy to keep secrets in the organization, and I don't think that does the job anyway. . . . Every president needs a good wife." "The silent language" is perhaps more readily understood by women (spouses, board members, secretaries, fellow administrators) than men.

Miriam Wood's own capacity for evocation as well as interpretation is evident in her book. It is not easy to combine materials drawn from a case study with tentative generalizations. Her fluency conceals artfulness. The work has increased my own sensitivity to the isolation of the college president and the presidential family. These individuals are rarely alone, but they have few people with whom they can be at ease. Presidents speak hauntingly for themselves in the pages of this book. One remarks warily, "What they do is raise your standard of living, get you dependent on them, and then you slowly do just what they want you to do. When I came here, I settled lightly. I can find other things to do." It is not only trustees one learns about here but also presidents, on whose resourcefulness and energy these private colleges heavily depend, and who in turn depend on the trustees in the best cases for intellectual exchange far more than for automatic support.

Acknowledgments

This book would not have been possible without the goodwill of the ten college presidents and forty trustees who received me with such courtesy in their homes and offices. To each of them, I once again express my thanks.

I am indebted to professors David Riesman, Nathan Glazer, Harold Howe II, and the late Stephen K. Bailey, all of Harvard University, for their support of this study. To Professor Emeritus Riesman I am especially indebted for correspondence sustained over a two-year period on the subject of trustees and presidents; his observations and counsel have been invaluable.

The manuscript was typed by Mrs. Shirley Howard of Chambersburg, Pennsylvania.

Introduction

This is a report of in-depth interviews with trustees and presidents from ten private liberal arts colleges located in four states. In confidential conversations with the chairman of the board of trustees, with three other members of the board, and with the college president, I have tried to develop a clear idea of what trustees actually do during the often substantial amounts of time they devote to college affairs. I have met with trustees in their homes and at their offices and have made notes of their responses to a series of open-ended questions such as, How would you describe the board's overall contribution to the operation of the college? and, How do you know whether or not the president is doing a good job? I have also met with each president in his office on campus and have asked similar questions in order to develop a sense of the president's perspective on the board's activities.

The point of these conversations has been to go beyond the formalities of charter and bylaws and to begin to understand the board's informal decision-making processes, its power structure, and its relations with the president. Only with this kind of information at hand can one begin to assess realistically both the potential and the limitations of the governing board as an institutional resource. A second objective of the study has been to provide an alternative to the treatment of trusteeship found in the literature on college governance. Articles and books written for board members' consumption tend to exhort trustees to comport themselves as key actors in the institutional drama, but in studies intended for scholars and administrators, trustees are often largely ignored. This volume, which is descriptive, tells how board members themselves perceive their role.

And finally, these conversations constitute a report on the status of American volunteerism and the lay governing board in the 1980s. It was Tocqueville who first pointed out the readiness of Americans to join together in support of the common good, and certainly the individuals who joined together as trustees to establish colleges are examples of this impulse. Yet times have changed, and in today's complex political and economic climate, it is legitimate to ask whether a well-meaning trustee, in his or her spare time, can responsibly "do good" on so large a scale as the smallest college has become.

Three colleges in the study have national reputations and are among the more academically selective in the country, and a fourth is on the fringes of eliteness with a strong regional reputation. The remainder of the colleges are in the middle ranges of competitiveness, four of them drawing about two-thirds of their students from the state in which the college is located.[1] Three of the colleges were founded in the late eighteenth century and are among the oldest in the nation, six were established during the waves of nineteenth-century religious evangelism, and one was organized early in this century. The endowments of the colleges range from a few million dollars to ninety million, with the two colleges at the upper end of the spectrum being considered very wealthy indeed.

On the whole, the campuses of these colleges are inviting places. The lawns, if not always sweeping, are spacious, and often there is a crisscross of well-trod pathways connecting buildings old and new, each of which seems to epitomize a prosperous period for the college— or for one of its donors. Occasionally, suburbia encroaches on the borders of the campus, and sometimes the town's commercial district has made its way to the college gates.

Not too long ago, these colleges typified the collegiate experience, but since World War II they have been engulfed by a public sector swollen by "baby boom" cohorts. As a result, although there are still 572 private, four-year liberal arts colleges, their enrollment represents only 4.8 percent of the total higher education enrollment; however, since each college has its own governing board, there are some 15,000 trustees involved in their governance. These colleges vary in size from less than 200 students to over 2,500 and differ as well in other important ways; for example, 55 percent of privately controlled four-year institutions have a Protestant or Roman Catholic religious affiliation. From among this variety I selected a homogeneous group: all ten colleges have student bodies between 1,000 and 2,500, all are nonprofit and officially nonsectarian, and all are coeducational and residential with a curricular emphasis on the liberal arts.[2] (See appendix 1 for further explanation.)

The governing boards of the colleges in this study are larger than many; on average they have thirty-four members each, compared with the national average of twenty-six for private, four-year accredited colleges. The largest board has fifty-six members, and the smallest has seventeen. The occupational characteristics of the trustees interviewed also vary substantially from the national averages for private college boards. Most notably, there are twice as many lawyers and retired persons as one would expect if the sample of trustees were exactly representative of the most recent gross national statistics. Business executives are underrepresented, with eleven in the sample compared with the fourteen expected according to national averages. As far as minority and female representation is concerned, there are seven women, all white, and one black man, whereas five women and two minority persons would be expected according to national averages for private colleges.[3]

Just as this trustee sample does not correspond exactly to national statistics, I doubt as well that it is in all ways representative of the 339 trustees serving these ten colleges. In selecting trustees to be interviewed, I depended upon the president for entrée. After meeting with the president, I asked if I might arrange additional interviews by writing directly to the board chairman, the chairman of a standing committee, and two other trustees the president might suggest who were not officers or committee chairmen. By talking with one or two trustees who were not on the Executive Committee, I hoped to get outside the ingroup that, I hypothesized, set the direction for every board, but in this I was only partially successful since, in almost every instance, the trustees with whom I spoke turned out to be "key" members of the board in one way or another. At the outset of the study, I surmised that presidents would naturally put me in touch with individuals who would respond positively to the request for an interview and would likely speak well of the college and of its president and board. This proved to be true, although as the interviews progressed I found that, with a single exception, each president had referred me to at least one trustee who, although very active, had something of the outsider's critical perspective, whether it might arise from being a female on a predominantly male board, a young alumna or alumnus on a predominantly older board, or a sharp-witted lawyer with a keen eye for human foibles.

What has emerged from these conversations is an impression of trustee activities at ten colleges during a nine-month period extending from May through January in the early 1980s. I call the results an "impression" rather than a "picture" because of the limitation of five interviews for each college. In my view, this shortcoming is balanced by the opportunity to compare the impressions thus gleaned from a total of ten institutions, and when I made this comparison, the themes addressed in this book—relations between board and president, operating styles of boards, the significance of the volunteer status of board members—emerged clearly from the data.

If, as I suspect, presidents were interested in my getting a relatively unvarnished impression of the board room, their interest may have arisen out of far from sanguine feelings about how their boards function and how the board and the president relate. This concern is well placed considering the dissatisfaction with presidential performance that existed at certain of these ten colleges during the period when the research took place. When I began the study, one board had just completed a full-scale review of the president. This review, which had involved trustees in on-campus interviews with faculty members, students, and staff, had resulted in a board decision to retain the president, and the board had subsequently embarked on a related "self-study" of its own activities. At another college, dissatisfaction with the president had led to the appointment of a trustee committee to oversee and advise him, and after a few months the board accepted the president's resignation. At a third college, a key trustee told me during our interview that he was trying to get support for a plan whereby the president would be asked to leave at the end of two years. These events suggest that in any given year, about 20 to 30 percent of boards will be dealing specifically with serious questions about the adequacy of the president's performance.

Because my interviews with trustees and presidents dealt in part with the sensitive subjects of presidential performance and the relationships between the president and the board and among board members, our conversations were conducted with the understanding that the identity of individual trustees and of their institutions would be disguised. Disguise has serious consequences in research because it lessens the public accountability that can be brought to bear on the researcher: the readers of these pages, except for the principals, who will of course recognize themselves and their own institutions, will not be able to check the impressions presented with their own perceptions of the governing boards at those institutions. Still, disguise has seemed imperative in a study that tries to get behind formalities and façades; few trustees or presidents would want to put their institution in a bad light by describing practices that might merit criticism. The method of disguise I have used here has involved withholding the exact dates of events, changing the names of presidents and certain particulars of their backgrounds, withholding the names of trustees and altering the occupational descriptions of those whose titles might identify them to a broad range of friends and business colleagues, and changing the geographic location of each college and distinctive features of its campus. In addition, I have given each college a false name and, except where a confidence would be betrayed, have attributed the comments of its president and trustees to the falsely named institution. This technique has the advantage of presenting the material in such form that a full case study of a single board can be reconstructed by going through chapter by chapter and drawing out material that I have organized according to my own thematic interests.

At the time of the interviews, a concern of those interviewed—and of mine—was the possibility that trustees and a president at a particular institution might be put in an embarrassing position with one another through an insensitive or ineptly organized presentation of the material. Of my success in avoiding this unfortunate outcome, the principals are the best judges, but I do find that the thematic presentation of material lessens these dangers and that, on the whole, the many quotations represent what the principals already know of one another's thinking.

The collegiate board rooms described here are typical of all boards in the evident preponderance of Caucasian men aged fifty and older, and it will be unfortunate indeed if the study perpetuates the status quo because it focuses on settings where the majority of the trustees and the president as well are white and male. In the text, I address the issue of women as trustees, but lacking data, I have nothing to offer on the important subject of minority participation in the board room. Furthermore, after some hesitation, I have decided not to identify repeatedly as a "black trustee" the one black trustee interviewed. It has seemed to me that this kind of nomenclature, although it would provide some small sense of a minority presence in the study, would place that trustee's comments in a context that significantly distorts my sense of our conversation.

As these latter remarks imply, various of a researcher's personal opinions and experiences may affect the ways in which data are presented and interpreted. In my own case, what is said in the following pages has been shaped by my work as an administrator, consultant, and faculty member in the collegiate setting and as a bureaucrat in a state education agency. A more direct influence has been service as a member of various boards: for two years I was a trustee of a private, four-year liberal arts college for women, and I have also served on the boards of a public university branch campus, a private community hospital, and a public community library; in the for-profit sector, I am a director of a closely held manufacturing firm.

I have brought to my research a sense that the board of a private college may do a great disservice to the institution by failing to focus specifically on the qualitative issue of how well people in the organization, particularly the president and board members themselves, are doing their jobs. In the absence of a climate in which conversations about the key issue of performance can be discussed nondefensively and with reasonable candor by board members and the president in the board room and by the president and senior administrators elsewhere within the organization, the exercise of trustee oversight can become a series of empty rituals. Some boards may prefer to facilitate these discussions through the use of outside experts who may be presidents or senior administrators working elsewhere but able to take the occasional extra assignment or who may be full-time professional consultants. Other boards may prefer to develop, on their own, procedures calling for periodic evaluative discussions with the president about the quality of the institution's leadership and about the success of the president and the board in fulfilling that responsibility. In either case, the value of the conversations will be enhanced if discussion about the quality of today's work is connected with a vision of the role the college will be playing in future years.

Of course, these views are inspired by an ideal of organizational life that, in practice, will never be attained. No matter how hard we try to rationalize the organization or to "humanize" its procedures, its processes of communication and decision making will remain somewhat of a muddle, and much of what we do will have outcomes quite different from what we intend. And we must acknowledge— even the most optimistic of us—that unplanned and unknown events taking place beyond the board room may overwhelm our best efforts to improve the stewardship of America's colleges. Still, I take it as an article of faith that coherence in organizational life and the desire to improve it are goals worth striving for in and of themselves. What may seem marginal changes at a single point in time in the confines of the board room are part of a continuum that, over a period of years, may have a major positive effect on the welfare of the college.

The plan of this book has been greatly influenced by my hope that it will find an audience not only among other students of higher education governance but also among trustees. In this spirit, part 1, The Board and the President, includes as chapter 1 a brief overview of the trustee mandate and role and a summary of recent attempts to redefine that role in light of a more complex social and economic environment and increasing demands for accountability. A recapitulation of the more widely disseminated models of campus governance is also included by way of orientation into the scholarly view of the campus milieu.

Then in chapter 2, How Boards Diminish the Presidency, and chapter 3, How Boards Evaluate the President, I plunge without further ado into what Stephen K. Bailey once termed "the most difficult, important, and complex relationship that boards have."[4] I have hoped that this approach will have three positive results: first, that the material will interest people and will immerse them in some of the complications which prompted the study; second, that the analysis will alert readers to some unintended consequences of the board-president relationship which they may not have recognized before; and third, that the use of the relationship between the board and the president to illustrate some of the pathologies of governing boards will encourage readers to go on to the following chapters, which contain a more systematic description of the interplay of structure, process, and trustee attitudes making boards vulnerable to these problems. Also in part 1, to demonstrate how difficulties between a board and a president may arise and to show how boards have tried to resolve them, chapter 4 includes case histories of the approaches taken by two boards to the evaluation of their presidents. A third "case" consists of the comments of a single trustee and is included because it captures at the point of germination an attempt to precipitate the resignation of a president.

In part 2, The Board as an Organizational Unit, I describe the board and its members as a discrete subunit of the collegiate organization, focusing on their status as volunteers and their reasons for serving and suggesting that the board's committee structure is the basis of an oligarchic distribution of power and influence among members. The financial activities of the board, considered by most trustees to be their most important obligation together with their responsibility to appoint and, if necessary, dismiss the president, are the subject of a separate chapter, as are the issues associated with the recruitment of trustees and the even more problematic issue of retiring them once their usefulness to the board has ended.

Part 3, Operating Styles of Boards, includes an elucidation of three models of board behavior. Each model reflects differing assumptions by trustees about the ways they properly relate to the president and to members of various campus constituencies as the board tries to meet its responsibilities for management of the college. Because a board's operating style influences its approach to policy making, this section also discusses the often ambiguous cleavage between *policy* and *administration* and suggests the concept of *policy structure* as a vehicle for more rational analysis of this often fuzzy distinction.

The concluding observations in part 4 set forth what I believe the analysis in the preceding sections suggests about the impact of the board upon the college and about its limitations and potential as an institutional resource. To increase the board's usefulness, both to the institution and to society-at-large, I suggest that trustees deemphasize their role as supermanagers and focus their attention on strate-gic questions, particularly on those issues in which there is a con-flict between institutional interests and the public interest, broadly conceived.

The appendixes include an elaboration of the methodology that guided the research and thumbnail sketches of the trustees, presidents, and colleges that are the subjects of this study. Citations appear at the end of the text, preceding the bibliography.

I The Board and the President

1 Governance in the Private Liberal Arts College

Paradoxically, it can be said of the United States' 572 private liberal arts colleges that they are similar but different. With student bodies typically ranging in size from five or six hundred to twenty-five hundred, they are remarkably alike as formal organizations. Each is headed by a president who, while accountable to a board of trustees, presides through a chain of command over an organizational hierarchy attenuated by guaranteed employment for tenured faculty. Similar in clientele, the majority of liberal arts colleges are coeducational and residential and cater principally to persons under the age of twenty-five. The chief formal difference among liberal arts colleges arises from their sectarian affiliation or lack of it.

Yet, quite apart from sectarian considerations, the distinctiveness of any individual campus will be loyally proclaimed by many an alumna or alumnus, by the president and members of the governing board, and also by certain faculty and students because of their perception that the college boasts, as one trustee puts it, "a special ingredient." Definitions of this ingredient will vary but generally include characteristics that exist independent of the college's formal organization. This perception of uniqueness is often associated with the personal interest expressed by faculty members in the students, the rigor of the course work, the friendliness of the students, or their diligence, or their intelligence. Then too, there are the more quantifiable factors: whether the college has a state, regional, or national student body; whether the faculty members pursued their graduate studies at elite universities and how many of them have attained the Ph.D.; whether the campus is located in the city or country; how wealthy and successful the alumni are, and so on.

In this environment, where relatively subtle qualitative differences determine a college's position in the constellation of kindred institutions, we do not often recall the starkness of the seventeenth century and the role the Puritans expected a college to play when, perched uncertainly on the edge of wilderness, they feared that heathenism and lawlessness might overtake their coming generations. A college, they felt, would provide their society with a bulwark against incipient barbarism and would serve as an enclave of piety and religious education. Although the colonists' intention had been to perpetuate the Oxford-Cambridge tradition in which final authority for the institution rested with the faculty, their sparse society lacked both the resources and the scholars to support spontaneous development of an institution of higher learning. As Frederick Rudolph observes, "A company of scholars could not assemble in the woods of Massachusetts without being called together by someone."[1] The Puritan solution to this problem was an act of the Massachusetts General Court appointing twelve of the most eminent men from throughout the colony as a Board of Overseers for Harvard College. Significantly, within a very few years the act was amended to clarify the responsibility of the Overseers to "dispose, order, and manage" the institution, thus establishing at the birth of American higher education that legal responsibility for management of a college would be vested in the governing board. Later, with the establishment of the College of William and Mary and of Yale College on similar principles of government sanction and absentee control, legal precedent and tradition were established: when a college was to be founded, a group of sponsors, usually not educators themselves, would seek governmental approval of an institution to be devoted not only to "the education of youth in the learned languages, the arts, and useful literature," as one nineteenth-century charter declares, but also to the advancement of Christian values.[2]

To provide for management of the college, the trustees customarily appointed a president who, by virtue of the office, assumed much of the board's formal authority. Under these circumstances the proper role of the board, once the founding of the college had been accomplished, was not clear. One outstanding president, Jasper Adams of Charleston College, spoke in 1837 of the "tendency to encroachment on the rightful sphere of the faculty [as] the besetting sin into which our boards of trustees have fallen, and to which they are always exposed."[3] Another nineteenth-century president, Francis Wayland of Brown University, wondered if trustees, ignorant as they were about both education and their institutions, were really necessary. If they are superfluous, he suggested, "the office which they hold had better be abolished."[4]

With a history of uncertainty associated with the trustee function, it is not surprising that the board's influence has decreased over time, first as presidential authority increased and later as faculty control over educational policy was secured. As a consequence, for the better part of this century, the trustee position has typically been one of "honorable obscurity," and the board's role has generally been construed to consist of making policy and delegating to the president and other administrators the functions of day-to-day management.

The formal structure and decision-making processes of collegiate governing boards, as set forth in bylaws, are remarkably similar. The bylaws describe a rationalized hierarchy with the chairman of the board at its apex and, in descending order of authority, the other officers of the board and then the chairmen of standing committees for finance, development, educational policy, buildings and grounds, and so on. This arrangement provides for decisions to be made when recommendations percolate up from committees to the full board; if recommendations are approved, they are to be implemented by the president of the college. Most bylaws stipulate that boards meet three or four times each year, presumably to direct their attention to financial affairs, other committee business and, when required, to the selection or termination of the president.

In recent years, however, questions have once again been raised— by the Carnegie Commission on Higher Education and other observers of higher education—about the proper functioning of the governing board.[5] During a period like the present, characterized by financial uncertainty and the specter of declining enrollments that threaten the welfare of all private colleges and the very viability of some, scholarly and general interest in trustees is heightened because how the college fares is ultimately the board's responsibility. What has not been clear is whether lay governing boards, as presently structured and operating, are in a position to play the policy-making role attributed to them and are able to exercise effective stewardship in a sometimes negative social and economic environment.

In defining a role for the governing board, the major theoretical issue revolves around how to marry the diverse and often conflicting notions underlying trusteeship. Abstract, exhortatory rhetoric is the usual means of reconciling these disparate elements, as is illustrated in this statement by the Carnegie Commission:

> It is more important for the board to provide for effective governance than, as it once did, to govern. . . . The board should neither abdicate its responsibilities to external or internal forces, nor bog itself down in details of administration. It should not run the college, but should assure that it is well run.[6]

However, a more lengthy treatment of the proper, or ideal, role for the board was written in 1975 by John Nason, former president of Swarthmore and Carleton colleges, under the auspices of the Association of Governing Boards of Universities and Colleges, a Washington-based interest group that serves a trustee clientele. This monograph and its revision published in 1982 are the only recent works attempting a comprehensive analysis of trustee responsibilities, and they are based on the assumptions "that the American pattern of lay trusteeship [will] continue, that many boards [are] not doing an adequate or effective job, and that the responsibilities of trustees will become more complex."[7] Also, it is anticipated that governing boards "will play a more important role in the years ahead than at any time in this century."[8]

In the 1982 monograph, Nason describes the ideal role of trustees by differentiating, for heuristic purposes, among thirteen responsibilities that range from six specific charges to broader, more abstract obligations. The six concrete duties include appointing the president, approving the budget, raising money, managing the endowment, approving the long-range plan, and serving as the court of appeal in matters of college governance. Five responsibilities are more general in nature and include making certain the institution is well managed, assuring adequate physical facilities, overseeing the educational program, serving as bridge and buffer between campus and community, and preserving institutional autonomy. The remaining two responsibilities deal with board members' attitudes toward the institution rather than actions to be taken; thus, trustees are urged to be informed about the "peculiar nature" of educational institutions, their own in particular, and to maintain the integrity of the trust.[9]

Nason also identifies fourteen factors that contribute to the effectiveness of boards. He cites the intangible characteristics of board morale and of trustee commitment to the institution as well as structural factors, such as the size of the board and the organization of its committees, and procedural factors, such as those regulating the composition of the board, the selection and orientation of its members, and the length of their tenure. Other factors identified as bearing on board effectiveness include the roles of the president and board chairman, the development of agendas, the frequency and length of meetings, and whether they are open or closed. Finally, boards are urged periodically to evaluate all of the institution's functions, including their own.

Overall, Nason's interpretation of trusteeship relies on a high order of interest, sensitivity, and judgment by individual trustees and by the board as a whole, particularly if oversight, which is recommended, is not to evolve into interference in administration, an outcome that both Nason and the Association of Governing Boards condemn. In explaining how trustees can meet his standard of care without intruding on administrative matters, Nason offers this advice:

> Trustees should be forever asking questions. Why this? Why that? This is not interference with administration. This is the kind of surveillance necessary to fulfill the trust committed to them.[10]

Rather than become enmeshed in administrative matters, trustees are advised to focus their attention on policy. Even then, according to another publication of the Association of Governing Boards, the trustees' involvement in the development of policy should take into account the prerogatives of the administration:

> The art of trusteeship consists largely of discovering and holding the middle ground of policy-making, eschewing with equal vigor the posture of mere validation on one hand and the usurpation of administration on the other.[11]

However the role of an individual trustee or the board as a whole unfolds in practice—and the variety of these roles is described in the following chapters—the fact remains that, in legal terms, the trustees as a group *are* the institution. In the college charter approved by the state legislature, the founders are listed by name and they and their successors are defined as the corporate body, making a board of trustees similar in this respect to the board of directors of a business corporation. Of special pertinence to this study, however, are the ways in which the boards of colleges differ from corporation boards, no difference being more important than the tradition in the not-for-profit sector of "lay" domination of the boards of control. This tradition holds that lay persons, or nonexperts, should be in charge of overseeing the efforts of professionals who are organized to serve the public. The theory is that lay boards of control, whether of schools, hospitals, community action agencies, or colleges and universities, are uniquely equipped to protect the public interest by assuring that the professionals and experts in these agencies do in fact contribute to the common good.

Although lay governance of education, whether of public schools or private colleges, is deeply embedded in American political custom, its effects on contemporary institutions have been little studied. More broadly, if the term *governance* is taken to refer to the interplay between the structure of an organization and the regularized processes, official and unofficial, by which the organization's members pursue that organization's stated ends, then it is only in very recent

years that the governance of higher education in any of its aspects
has been studied systematically, and the emphasis in that research
has been on the processes for decision making. Little scholarly effort
has been focused on elucidating the role of the governing board;
rather, the object of research has been to describe the relationship
between the faculty and administration, both on the small college
campus and in large, centralized systems, and to understand how
leadership, especially presidential leadership, is exercised in these
milieus.[12]

Among the numerous descriptions, or models, of campus governance which have been proposed in the course of this research, four
are of interest here because they provide useful insights into the
workings of colleges and universities and together suggest something
of higher education's organizational complexity. Of these models, the
most venerable likens the college or university to a collegium in which
the professional authority of the faculty is virtually inviolate and
decision making occurs through consensus between faculty and
administration. The president of the college in this metaphor functions as the *primus inter pares* in an organization of professionals. In
a second model, the college is visualized as an academic bureaucracy,
where the participants occupy places in a formal hierarchy that
operates on the basis of official policies and rules. In this model, the
president is more than the first among equals; he or she is a
commanding figure who stands atop a bureaucratic pyramid and
wields much of the organization's power. A third and more recently
developed model pictures the college as a political system and posits
the existence of interest groups on campus with differing goals.
According to this model, conflict among the groups is the normal
state of affairs, and the president's role is to function as a mediator.

The fourth and most provocative model was developed by Michael
D. Cohen and James G. March, who, in a study of college and
university presidents and their styles of leadership, found that decision
making takes place under conditions of "organized anarchy."[13] In
their view, rational decision making—weighing the alternatives and
making the most favorable choice—is precluded in the collegiate
setting because the goals of the organization are "inconsistent and ill-
defined." The processes of teaching and learning, which are the
"technology" of the organization, are "familiar [but] not understood,"
and the participants phase in and out of the process and differ in
the amount of time they are willing to devote to solving problems.
In this environment, problems and their solutions become separated
in time and organizational space, and the president's role is to keep
track of useful solutions and to pursue them in whatever context

they happen to appear. In such a setting, the president who conceives of himself or herself as operating in either a bureaucratic or political role will miss opportunities for achieving desirable goals.

While the accuracy of these metaphors might be disputed in whole or in part, their variety is useful in suggesting how little consensus there is about the role of the president, who is the board's agent on campus. Furthermore, it is interesting that throughout the history of American higher education, the power of the college presidency has been variable, ebbing and flowing in relation to the power of the board and of the faculty and students, although from time to time at most liberal arts colleges the president has cast a very long shadow— one thinks of Donald John Cowling who presided at Carleton College from 1909 to 1945 or of William T. Foster's influence in establishing Reed College as an institution of the first rank. Recently, however, there have been few presidents who have appeared to their contemporaries to be larger than life, the last of the powerful presidents of long tenure and heroic image having retired in the 1950s and 1960s.

At the present time, it seems that on the private college campus, as in the society at large, leadership in the heroic mode is somehow irrelevant. And although board members' rhetoric sometimes suggests otherwise, trustees today do not usually expect the college presidency to be a position of power for an individual who expresses strong views about higher education, the future of the liberal arts curriculum, or the maintenance of academic standards. Such an individual would alienate important constituencies—the faculty, the students, the alumni, or even some trustees. What is required instead is a person who, in the words of one chairman of the board, is at once "an academician, social butterfly, and administrator."

2 How Boards Diminish the Presidency

A college president's first acquaintance with members of the governing board frequently occurs during the presidential search, and trustees who have recruited a new president are conscious that the search is fueled in part by rhetoric that no candidate is actually expected to embody. As the board chairman at Salinger College observes:

> We start out looking for a president, we want him to be brilliant, attractive, handsome, with a beautiful wife, happily married, with nerves of steel, a great statesman and money-raiser, with academic credentials to impress the faculty, young ideas that make him popular with the students, endurance to go day and night, naturally good health, fine morals, [and] impeccable credentials.

Irony notwithstanding, this is a telling description. Perhaps most arresting in this conception of the presidency, aside from the assumption that the president will be a he, is the implication that image is more important than substance. Academic credentials are valued for their usefulness in impressing the faculty, not for what they suggest about the president's qualities of mind or ideas about higher education, while ideas are important in eliciting a positive response from the students and are valued when they increase the popularity quotient. So pervasive is the notion of image that the chairman at Faulkner College adds, "Style is important, personal appearance—does he look presidential?" Yet from the trustee perspective, this emphasis on surface effects is simply an inevitable corollary to the set of competing expectations and biases espoused by faculty members and students. During the search, these expectations are the subject of bargaining and trade-offs by representatives of the various college constituencies appointed to the presidential search committee, thus assuring the board that the candidates brought to them meet some standard of acceptance for all parties involved.

The Second-Best President

Not surprisingly, the candidate who emerges as the first choice through this process of compromise may not correspond to the candidate most favored by the board members themselves, a circumstance that seems to contribute to the faint air of disappointment—the presumption that the president may somehow be second-best—which is detectable in the conversation of some trustees. Not infrequently, for instance, trustees will give way during the selection process to the sentiments of the faculty, as this board chairman recalls:

> When our current president came to be interviewed, I liked him well enough, but I would have picked the guy from ————. But surprisingly, the faculty went for [the current president], and . . . I went along.

But even after the compromises have been made and the search committee has agreed on its first choice, the preferred candidate may decline, prompting a board member at one prestigious college to remark that "poor [current president] came in second in our search ten years ago and this time too." And a trustee at yet another college, who admits that his own relative youth and inexperience may have inflated his good opinion of a previous president, says of the present president:

> I personally think the previous president was a better college president than our current one, but I only saw the last eighteen months of the previous president's ten years. Our current president has grown enormously in the job and quite possibly a new trustee would feel the same way about a successor to the current president.

The origin of trustees' feelings that a president is not quite up to standard varies from individual to individual and from institution to institution; even so, the existence of an undercurrent of disappointment may help to explain why so few trustees express spontaneous enthusiasm about the incumbent president and about what that person might accomplish for the college. It is unusual for trustees to be as enthusiastic as the Poe College board member who, when asked to describe the college's two or three biggest problems, replies: "If we lost [the president]—the fact that he's good is known—worries me. I don't think he's easily replaceable." At Frost College, the chairman remarks of the sixty-year-old president of long tenure, "I dread his ever leaving the school." Far more typical, however, are the sentiments of the board chairman at Salinger, who offers thoughtful but measured praise of a president who has been in office for nearly a decade: "We think well of the president, but we don't expect him to be a miracle man. He's a good operator, a practical administrator. He's a good president and has served us well."

The College Presidency as a Political Office

To describe a president as a "good operator" is to signal that politics and political metaphors are not confined to the presidential search. Indeed, trustees and experienced presidents say that the college presidency is in some measure a political office, as this Faulkner board member makes clear:

> It's a political position as well as an academic one. In fact, it's highly political. You have such diverse constituencies. You have to satisfy so many constituencies, and they are all antagonists: the faculty wants more money; the administration wants more; the faculty in each department want the money to go to them.

As these comments suggest, the realities of incumbency require a president with the skills and temperament to keep the college's constituencies in a reasonable state of satisfaction, leading a Twain College trustee to observe, "The test of skill of a president is how he can be a master of the dialogue and lead disparate groups." A strong sense of the political role flavors the conversation of presidents, too, and the president of Salinger remarks in passing, "People think presidents have power, but they are power brokers." In a similar vein, the president of Poe College has identified fourteen constituencies whose interests he must consider, including not only the faculty, students, administrators, trustees, alumni, parents, and townspeople, but also prospective students, presidential peers, scholarly peers, foundations, state government, the federal government, and corporations. So influential are these various interest groups that the president of Faulkner has found that college presidents "can be leaders only in the political sense," and he has concluded that, in our present environment, "we have diminished the extent to which a college administrator can be an educational leader."

For a college president, one implication of being a politician and a power broker who mediates among various constituencies is that adopting firm and unequivocal positions on contested issues may eventually result in one's credibility, or even one's job, being on the line. A Twain trustee tells the poignant story of a previous president who expressed strong opinions on matters considered controversial on campus and among the alumni, and he recalls his own efforts to educate that president to the political realities of a small college:

> Usually we stayed up after the meeting and had a few Scotches, and the burden of my remarks was, don't go up front on this. Let the committee write the report; if they fracture, they fracture. Get the hell away from the front line.
> And he went up front and he is blamed.

This president, according to another member of the board, ultimately alienated so many alumni with his "up front" positions that the college's fund-raising capacity was seriously impaired, and he submitted his resignation.[1]

The College President as Bureaucrat

Although the president's political role as a broker of diverse and conflicting views is informally recognized in the college board room, the board's formal relationship to the president is based on a quite different—and logically incompatible—assumption. This premise is that the college as an organization is a rational hierarchy with the president occupying a position at the top of a bureaucratic pyramid from which power radiates downward. Boards and presidents have long related to one another on this basis, but in recent years the board's bureaucratic processes have become increasingly important as trustees have found themselves accountable for difficult decisions about how to effect economies. At the same time, the continuation in the broader society of an information explosion has meant that more and more board members have come to expect—and many presidents have become eager to provide—extensive background documentation not only about budget, endowment, and maintenance, which are traditional areas of trustee interest, but now also about issues such as tenure ratios, admissions programs, and forward planning. As a result, the paper work of most private college boards is substantial. Memorandums and statistics, not to mention financial reports, are generally mailed to members in advance of meetings, so that the very act of coping with the paper tends to focus board members' attention almost exclusively on bureaucratic outcomes, whether these be quantifiable results in admissions or fund raising or a review of specific administrative programs. In fact, unless a board meeting coincides with the commencement or alumni weekends, when the president may customarily make an address both academic and inspirational in tone, trustees may have relatively meager exposure to the president in a role other than that of top-level, bureaucratic functionary.

Symbolic of the bureaucratic influence in the board room at many colleges is the appropriation from business and government of the managerial tool of annual or strategic planning. At Melville College, where planning is envisioned by the president and board chairman as a way of arriving at priorities for a three-year period, the president explains that "the chairman is very strong on planning and has led the administration and board into a whole new procedure." The board chairman, who in his professional life is president of a Fortune 500 company, says that the board sees itself as "the elicitor of the president's plan," and he goes on to mention "significant initiatives" that the planning process has helped to formulate, including a recruiting program based on sophisticated demographic data, a major fund drive, and new arrangements for managing the college properties and other capital resources.

Of course, the existence of an elaborate plan is not required to reveal the managerial viewpoint of the many trustees who devote much of their attention to the administrative aspects of the presidency. At Thoreau College, one trustee wants a report from the president on "enrollment and significant [administrative] resignations," while at Cather, concern is expressed about "cost considerations . . . as well as enrollment which could go down in the next decade . . . and maintaining the properties." And always important to trustees as a basic index of institutional health are the annual financial results, prompting one president to remark, only half-joking: "The bottom line—that's all they question. They're only interested in whether it's in the black."

A trustee at Salinger is unusual in her negative reaction to this bureaucratic emphasis. She remarks that "college trusteeship is made too easy" and says that what trustees should be thinking about are the "difficult questions: Well, what about the next decade? What direction should the college be going in? Are we prepared to give up liberal arts and start vocational courses? What do we mean by liberal arts?" Occasionally, this trustee continues, the discussion at board meetings will broaden to encompass such issues, but "people get squirmy, and when good things happen, because of time limitations, they don't happen." Similarly, a trustee at Cummings College is thinking of the broader issues left undiscussed when she concludes that "it's hard to keep time for both maintenance and looking ahead, thinking ahead."[2]

In this atmosphere, where board members have become accustomed to behaving as if the college were a bureaucracy and the president the chief bureaucrat, it is not surprising that boards do not often address themselves to overarching questions of institutional mission, nor do they spend much time discussing the abstract and elusive concept of educational leadership. Although most trustees would be hard put to disagree with the Thoreau board member who says the president's province is "to help promote, change, and help the place grow better," in most board rooms this expectation, together with the implied question of whether the board would support a president interested in broad questions of educational change and improvement, is overwhelmed by the urgency associated with the quest for balanced budgets, steady enrollments, and controlled tenure levels.

The President and the Board's Committee System

While on the one hand the managerial interests of the board tend to cast the president in the role of chief bureaucrat, on the other hand the committee activities of the board have the effect of subtly devaluing the contribution of the president in comparison with the senior staff. In the extreme case, the president may seem almost expendable—or at least somewhat extraneous to the efficient workings of the trustee committee system. At the heart of the board's committee structure are the standing committees, such as the Committee on Finance and the Committee on Academic Affairs, which correspond to the college's administrative functions. The president generally delegates much of the research and paper work for a committee to a senior administrative officer, and customarily a member of the senior staff is in attendance at trustee committee meetings so that the president is able to tailor his or her degree of active involvement as issues and circumstances may dictate.

One result of these arrangements is that the president, in comparison to the senior staff, may be a less familiar personality to many trustees. More significantly, the president's activities may seem less germane to the immediate welfare of the college than those of the senior staff, because what the president does is not as conspicuously demonstrable to the board as, for example, are the accomplishments of a vice-president for finance who devises the budget and works closely with the Committee on Finance in overseeing the board's investments. A committee chairman typically relies heavily on the staff member assigned to the committee, and since this dependence encourages frequent communication, the trustee-staff relationship commonly becomes quite close, as suggested by the chairman of the Salinger College Development Committee:

I'm in touch with the vice-president for development constantly. He's my
key source, and we're in communication once a week and sometimes
more. . . . I may talk with the president once a month, and I see him at
Executive Committee once a month.

A committee chairman may also feel that the president does not
really have time to spare for the details of committee business and
that, although the president must be kept properly informed, the
trustees and senior staff do best by working independently to see
that everything gets accomplished, as this chairman of the Twain
Development Committee explains:

————— and ————— are our line people [to work with]; clearly the
president has enough to do. All of the capital campaign I do directly
with the vice-president for resources, and only those things he should be
brought up to date on is the president involved in.

Sometimes a tacit understanding springs up between a committee
chairman and a staff member regarding the president's opinions and
sensitivities, so that a board member may feel somewhat in league
with the staff member, as inferred by this chairman of an Educational
Policy Committee:

Our academic dean is easy to work with. In talking about a committee
agenda, I can say, "This would upset [the president], but we have to do
it anyway," and this is accepted by [the academic dean] as a direct
statement, not as undercutting the president.

Thus confidence in a staff member's discretion, as well as admiration
and respect for that individual, can be a by-product of committee
activity. (Occasionally, of course, familiarity is the basis for thinking
less well of a staff person, as in the case of the Poe College trustee
who describes one senior administrator as "competent but a little
cavalier in his methods.")
    But when trustees' admiration for the occupants of the vice-
presidential level grows without a corresponding increase in good
feeling for the president, a trustee may muse about the president's
usefulness, as has this Cummings trustee: "Maybe Cummings College
doesn't need a president. A college can run very effectively with the
top administrators and the [senate of] the faculty." This reaction,
however, is extreme. In practice, the result of trustees' admiration
for a particular senior staff member is likely to be more restrained
although still significant, as at Melville, where the business manager's
salary has been taken out of the hands of the president and is decided

directly by the trustee Compensation Committee. At Twain, a greatly admired vice-president is described as "talented" and "equivalent to the executive vice-president of the college" and is such a key figure that the board chairman involves him as "part of my conversations with the president, which take place once a week or every other week."

A rather dramatic example of staff members overshadowing the president occurred at Cather College several years ago when the president was in his second year. The senior staff was comprised of holdovers from the previous administration, and according to the present chairman of the board:

> There were no guys on the administrative staff loyal to the new president. The business manager was the tool of a trustee, and the academic dean was under the control of [a faculty member who had influence with several members of the board]. . . .
>
> [Since the then-board chairman was ill] and the whole thing was so critical, I got members of the senior staff together and told them to work together as a group. . . . It was a matter of letting the staff know who is boss. . . . It was just a period of testing of the new president. These meetings established the new president as boss.

In this case, well-established relationships involving trustees, administrators, and faculty have apparently been successfully rechanneled within the president's purview, and the chairman now "can't believe how well things are running."

Two presidents, obviously sensitive to the potential for being outshone or outflanked by their staffs, spoke specifically of trying to keep abreast of trustee-staff relationships, with the president of Poe remarking that "on substantial issues, the board chairman does not see anyone on campus without my knowledge." At Frost College, where the chairmen of standing committees speak frequently on the telephone with staff members, the president makes a point of attending standing committee meetings, although senior staff are present, so that the trustees "can use the president to support their ideas." Then at monthly meetings of the Executive Committee, when the president and the various trustee committee chairmen sit around a table, the president maintains eye contact with his staff members, who are seated off to one side. If a trustee asks anyone but the president a question, he expresses displeasure: "There is good reason for this: I am freer to disclose information, and [as president] you have to constantly demonstrate that you know what's going on." This president laughed about "revealing myself " by admitting the continual pressure he feels to demonstrate to trustees his complete control of the organization. But he clearly meant for the admission to be taken as evidence of a conscious strategy for maintaining his preeminence as the most knowledgeable, and least dispensable, employee of the college.

3 How Boards Evaluate the President

For a significant minority of presidents, incumbency—now estimated to average seven years—sooner or later brings a serious crisis in which the board questions whether it is desirable for the president to continue in office.[1] During the May through January period covered by this study, one president resigned under board pressure and left the campus in the middle of the academic year, another had just emerged from a campuswide appraisal personally conducted by members of the governing board, and at a third college, one trustee described how he was trying to garner support among fellow board members to engineer the resignation of the president. As the president of Faulkner observed three days after his own resignation had been announced:

> One of the interesting things about all this: I called around to my buddies and it's incredible how many have the same kinds of problems. . . . It's more common than not that boards and presidents have differences. If you get underneath, you find a lot of stirring.

These symptoms of uneasiness at the uppermost level of the organization are by no means unique to higher education. Not too long ago, the *New York Times Magazine* ran a cover story entitled "Executive Anxiety: Why Big Business Is Firing the Boss," in which it was asserted that "a new and edgy atmosphere haunts America's executive suites."[2] In *The New Republic,* an article on "America's Management Crisis" pointed out that the tenure of chief executive officers now averages just five years,[3] and *Business Week* concluded that "turnover at the top is hitting levels without precedent in recent history."[4] Clearly, any uncertainties in the relationship between the president and the trustees in the board rooms of higher education are part of a pattern found elsewhere in society.

In the private college sector, it is not customary to establish explicit procedures and criteria for evaluating the president, although many trustees maintain that hiring and, if necessary, firing the president is their primary responsibility. Although formal programs of executive evaluation have been widely adopted in business, government, and public higher education, most of the governing boards in this study continue to rely on informal procedures.[5] If official conversation with the president about the caliber of his work does occur, it usually takes place in conjunction with an annual adjustment in the president's compensation, although here, too, there seems to be a feeling among some trustees that the amount of the salary increase tells a president all he needs to know about his standing with the board.

Significantly, the process of evaluating the president throws into high relief a problem which lies at the heart of absentee oversight, namely, How can trustees arrive at an independent judgment about the president's competence in the performance of duties when the president, as the board's agent on campus, is the trustees' official source of information on all institutional matters? That there is not unanimity of opinion about how this issue is properly resolved will be evident in the observations of the trustees who are quoted in the following pages. In general, however, it can be said that roughly three-quarters of those interviewed feel that in order to evaluate the president's performance with reasonable accuracy, they need to have sources of information independent of the president.

As to the criteria against which the president's performance is to be judged, many trustees seem uncertain about what standards to apply once the evaluation moves from a consideration of quantitative bureaucratic outcomes, such as whether the budget is balanced and how much the alumni fund has increased, to a consideration of the qualitative characteristics of performance, which trustees often refer to as "style." Few trustees have defined explicitly in their own minds the qualitative criteria which underlie their judgments of the president, perhaps because they instinctively feel that such definitions are problematic at best. A Thoreau trustee with long experience as a university president ruminates:

> What kind of scorecard do you make for a president? Each president has his style. Former President ───────── [of Thoreau] wouldn't be comfortable in these days. You have to evaluate every man in his context.
>
> Are trustees smart enough to make a scorecard? . . . No one can develop a tool for measuring presidential performance since the presidents have different talents and the institutions different demands.

The belief that each presidency must be considered on its own terms is shared by many board members, and trustees working within such a fluid value system often find, as a former chairman of the Twain board remarks, that it is easier to spot a bad relationship between a president and a college than it is to figure out what makes a good one.

Sources of Information about the President

Part of the board's problem in evaluating the president arises because facets of the presidency which an absentee board directly observes consist principally of the reports generated for trustee consumption and the way the board itself is handled. Under these circumstances, a trustee at Faulkner College feels that the board meeting is an "excellent" opportunity for trustees to make judgments about

> sound development of the budget, how policy is to be implemented, and whether the president is poorly prepared or a muddle-head.
>   We are *not* in a position to evaluate how he runs the administration or how he runs the faculty meeting. If oversight boards get into that, then we are meddling.

According to this view, the president is the official channel of communication between members of the board and everyone on campus (except for the senior administrators assigned to deal directly with committee members). More specifically, when a trustee and dean or faculty member talk together about the president's activities and campus events, especially in critical fashion, the faculty member or dean might be accused of "telling tales out of school" and the trustee of failing to be properly supportive of the president. To avoid overstepping these boundaries is very important to about one-quarter of the trustees interviewed, and they would agree with the board chairman at Poe:

> I don't interfere. People [from campus and the town] say you ought to do this or that, and I say that's for [the president] to decide. . . .
>   As for the rest of it, the internal matters— if something were out of line, I feel sure I'd hear about it. Members of the staff make reports, and we have to make a judgment about that. Really, judging the president is based on being with him and what I can hear.

The majority of trustees interviewed, however, express a desire to have avenues of information independent of the president, and most of them rely on the student newspaper as a major resource. While trustees are at pains to discount the newspaper's accuracy ("I was a student once, too") and its biases ("It does give an idea of the student and faculty view"), most of them take it seriously as a description of sentiments on campus, and from time to time issues raised in the newspaper stimulate board action. At Cather College, for example, newspaper articles played a role, if they did not cause, trustee intervention to shore up a weakened president. But for the most part, trustees read the student newspaper with a certain skepticism, as the remarks of a Frost College trustee suggest: "I look at the college newspaper. It has plenty of digs at the president, dean, and others, but these are not abnormally high and are of no consequence." The town newspaper is also a source of information for certain trustees, usually those living near the college, and one board member at Poe wonders "how trustees who don't read the local paper know what's going on."

More persuasive than either the student or town newspaper in influencing what trustees think of the president is the "rumor mill." "You have to listen to the rumor mill," say both a veteran trustee at Cummings and a younger trustee at Poe. Even so, how to treat the rumor mill—through which flows shoptalk, hunches, gossip, and scuttlebutt originating mainly in the faculty—is a delicate matter, as indicated by a Cummings trustee who has a number of friends among the faculty and administration: "I am torn about how much to listen to what I hear from them and how much to try to develop more sources. I could make phone calls to the campus and I never have." In the case of a Thoreau trustee who is active in alumni affairs, special phone calls are unnecessary because she is on campus frequently and, without making any particular effort, can easily pick up on the campus grapevine:

> It is easier to tell if a president is good at a small school. Faculty reaction is a prime consideration, and there are still some faculty there who were there when I was. There are different jobs to do with the alumni association and through those I've gotten reacquainted. And I see a few faculty at social events and meet the newer faculty through trustee committees.

Among the board members who appear least affected by the "rumor mill" are the trustees at Frost, where the board's contacts with faculty are limited to a few select committee meetings and an annual dinner. Although this arrangement seems quite satisfactory to three of the Frost trustees interviewed, one board member seems regretful and just a bit wary that the president might be trying to keep faculty members and trustees apart:

> I have a few friends on campus, but I don't solicit their views; I don't intend to be a snooper, and I don't look for complaints. . . .

I don't feel that I should have contact with the faculty. I don't see anything wrong with trustees talking with faculty and students, but the president and perhaps the dean might prefer not, and I don't.

Among those trustees who find they cannot be satisfied by the formal channels of communication, several mention feeling somewhat uncomfortable with members of the faculty; for them, a confidential relationship with an administrator may be preferable, as is the case with a Cather trustee who relies on similar informal relationships in running his small grocery store chain:

My source of information is [a senior administrator]. Every trustee should have some source like that. You have to have your own people just the way I call my assistant manager at our store in ———— once a month.

Often relationships with staff members are limited to the one or two administrators whom a trustee gets to know through committee activities, but occasionally a trustee has a veritable network of inform- ants and exudes a perfect confidence that he or she knows what is taking place on campus and how the president is faring, as does this trustee, also at Cather:

I have [more sources of information about the college] than most. Let's see, I get the minutes of the weekly administration meeting, and the college paper; I visit the campus twice, maybe three times a month for committee meetings and for sports events except in the winter when I'm away. And there's the college quarterly. And the telephone. I talk with coaches, the dean and maybe the president or business manager. And I have lots of friends on the faculty, and I see students from town here.

Although most board members find their links with the campus to be less numerous and often more tenuous than those of this trustee, they nevertheless say again and again, with the certainty of a board member from Salinger, "Where there is concern [about the president], I receive unofficial communication."

Problems Inhibiting Communication about Presidential Performance

Although a number of trustees use the term *style* to describe how the intangibles of personality, appearance, academic and social back- ground, and manner of exercising authority bear on administrative effectiveness, no one seems to know how to discuss these issues in a

businesslike way in the board room or in private with the president.
Such discussions, if they occur at all, take place individually, perhaps
"over a few Scotches" or on the telephone, as when a Cather trustee
tries to reassure a president who refers to himself as an "outsider"
by replying, "That's why you're there." Yet because trustees find it
difficult to talk with a president about management style and the
president's "fit" with the campus, and because they may feel that
information from the rumor mill and the student newspaper is biased
and perhaps not a legitimate basis for official discussion, a board's
developing concerns about a president may not surface either in the
course of the official work of the board or in the relatively infrequent
executive sessions held by most boards. Nor are these trustee criticisms
always clearly intuited by the president; most often they remain an
undercurrent, discussed sotto voce among the active and influential
members.

Midst these currents of feeling and perception, a board's communication with the president about how his or her work is progressing
often falls into the ambiguous pattern described by a trustee at
Melville College:

> I don't think the board is even involved in performance evaluation. The
> Executive Committee approves things on a regular basis and we review
> the president's salary on occasion. . . .
> The president came on board, and we gave him two or three years,
> and two years ago we were not happy and we conveyed that impression
> by body English, and there has been marked improvement over the past
> year.

I asked what was entailed in communicating with "body English":
"Well, we conveyed our dissatisfaction by the questions we would
ask." Body language as a mode of communication is by no means
unique to Melville. The president of Frost College says he knows
what has been going on by the way trustees are sitting when he comes
into the room, especially at that time of year when his compensation
is discussed. "You have to read that silent language," he says.

In the meantime, the words spoken and the "official" attention of
the board and the president are focused on discussible bureaucratic
issues, whether these be quantifiable results in admissions or fund
raising or a review of specific administrative programs or an assessment of the president's overall role in seeing that favorable institutional results are achieved, as described by this Cummings College
trustee:

> The points you usually look to are, Is the college attracting the students

it wants and the faculty? Is the operation in the black? Is he a good salesman outside? Is he a successful fund-raiser?

Other points you might look to are, How about applications for admission? What is the quality of his administrative appointments? How good is he at channeling resources—that's resourcefulness.

In this atmosphere, made ambiguous by a mix of implicit and explicit expectations, it is not surprising that presidents vary in their impressions of their own individual scorecards. A president may sense that the standards are largely managerial, as at Frost where the president, believing that "trustee thinking about the college is influenced by their own perceptions about their own business," feels it imperative to attend to, and demonstrate mastery over, such financial matters as "quick ratios, assets, fund balances, [and] deferred maintenance." At Melville and Longfellow, too, the presidents have concluded that the scorecard is largely managerial, and each seems to feel that he is somehow immune to the bad effects of criticism if he adheres to the annual plan, as the president of Melville suggests: "The planning process determines priorities, and I can't be taken to task so long as I'm in concert with them." Similarly, the Longfellow president sees the annual plan as "cut[ting] out the cheap shots" of members who would take him by surprise with expectations and objectives he has not agreed to in advance.

A president may also intuit that the scorecard demands most of all a certain style, as is the case at Thoreau, where the president feels that "a strong presidency is seen as key by the board." But for other presidents, the mix of stated and unstated expectations can be more confusing, as at Cummings, where the president says "it took me a while to locate my style with the board." And at Faulkner, the president's misunderstanding of the scorecard was an important factor in his resignation, as he himself observes: "I thought the board wanted a president-provost, not a fund-raising president and someone good at holding hands with the governing board."

The idea that a process of formal evaluation might help to clarify the sometimes murky relations between board members and the president meets with little enthusiasm, especially among board chairmen, who would be expected to play the central role in discussing an evaluation face-to-face with the president. Several agree with the chairman of the Twain board:

I don't think formal performance evaluation is desirable. The opportunity for board members to discuss performance comes up in the spring when we go into executive session to talk about compensation. It's up to the chairman to take the lead in this, and I'd prefer not to do it under a rigorous basis.

A "rigorous basis," he goes on to say, might be unduly stressful for a president, and he adds, a college has certain "institutional ambiguities" that make a rigid management-by-objectives performance review inappropriate. At Melville College the board chairman, himself the chief operating officer of a large, multinational corporation, worries that performance standards could be inadvertently misapplied by board members who "don't understand participatory management" and the limitations it puts on the president:

> Some trustees have unrealistic expectations. They really, I think, are too limited in their exposure to organizations that involve professional management. I sense a too limited exposure and that they imagine that the president in general plays a larger role and is more omnipotent than in fact he is. And because of this unrealistic view, they have an unrealistic expectation of what presidents can do.

Only two chairmen seem to be confident that formal evaluation may have intrinsic values that outweigh its drawbacks. One of the two is from Cummings, where complaints through the "rumor mill" ultimately prompted the trustees to undertake a full-scale administrative review of the president. As a result of that experience, the chairman reports, the board

> did authorize the [board] chairman, vice-chairman, and the chairman of the Administrative Review Committee to do an annual review and to take it back to the Executive Committee. We have decided that every year the president will first present his review of the year and then the Executive Committee will go into executive session [for further discussion]. It's good to have it automatic and annual.

At Longfellow, the chairman has enthusiastically introduced evaluation procedures that have worked well in the large corporation where he is chief legal counsel. He expects the president to come to the Executive Committee in September with "goals and objectives" for the coming year and a "performance report" on the year just completed; these procedures seem to him to be perfectly straightforward and workable.

At the majority of colleges in the study, however, the board's reliance on informal methods of evaluation persists. Thus, the customs at Salinger College are typical not only because they seem haphazard but also because, among the trustees and the president, there are differing perceptions about what is taking place. The president, who has been in office for ten years, says there is no evaluation of his activities "except what comes along with my salary discussions," and then he adds wryly, "and a lot of times trustees forget the president's pay raise!" Nonetheless, this president feels he is subjected to an evaluative process in the Executive Committee in the course of its ongoing conversation with him about college affairs. The chairman of the board, who has a close working relationship with the president and is in touch with him at least twice a week, has a view of performance evaluation almost identical to that of the president:

> No, there are no formal procedures. Our contact in Executive Committee with the president is so frequent that we don't formally review his performance. We know on a monthly basis how things are going, so there would be nothing to say except that we want to hold on to him.

Another member of the same Executive Committee, however, describes the presidential evaluation procedure quite differently, recalling an established process:

> I don't think the procedures are written down, but yes, it's done by the Executive Committee. Once a year it reviews the entire picture, financially mainly, but it reviews the president's performance, how he has done this past year.
> The chairman has a conversation with the president very thoroughly right before the June meeting, when there is an executive session of the Executive Committee and a discussion of his performance for the past year. Then there's a report to the full board; we say we've gone through these items and then anyone can say "I don't like what we did here." The raise is discussed and there is a vote.
> Several years ago, three or four people took care of all this, and the rest of the board didn't know what was going on, but for four or five years there has been more formality. Once, two years ago, the Executive Committee was of mixed mind, and the whole plan changed in board meeting.

Two other Salinger trustees express a third point of view. Neither is a member of the Executive Committee, and both say that they are not informed about whether, or by whom, the president may be evaluated. Says one:

> I'm not sure that the board does have a formal procedure for evaluating the president. Maybe the Executive Committee has a procedure, but I'm not aware of a report brought back to be shared. Of course, what's happening to the school is itself an evaluation—the number going on to graduate school, the job placement, the number of Phi Betes.

And another says:

> There's never been a time the president has left a board meeting.
> There's no five- or ten-year evaluation process so far as I know. If there
> is, it's done in private, and those are councils I'm not privy to. I imagine
> his salary raises would come up in the Committee on Finance.

Similar differences in perception among board members about how
or whether the president's competence is periodically evaluated exist
in six of the ten boards in the study. At these colleges, however, the
absence of clear-cut procedures for talking about how the president
is doing his job does not seem to have produced any outwardly
detrimental effect. The colleges continue to thrive, and where differences of opinion may exist about how well the president is
performing, these differences have not surfaced in ways that presidents and trustees describe as a problem.

A significant feature of trustee thinking about evaluation of the
president is their assumption that performance appraisal connotes
censure primarily, and a board chairman may worry about the effect
negative comments would have on the president. "Being president is
tough enough," says the Twain chairman, adding that evaluation "is
not a matter for the spotlight," the implication being that coping with
negative feedback is more than an overburdened president should
be asked to endure. A similar fear of hurting the president's feelings
causes the Melville chairman to have qualms about the more formal
evaluation process now being urged upon him by two or three
members of the Executive Committee:

> There is danger that the president will misread what we say as criticism
> and that he will feel anxiety. It's my intention to say that this is our way
> of doing things, that we have our foibles. If it strikes him as high-
> handed, then it stands to reason it will be misunderstood.

It also appears that the process of presidential evaluation is a
potential source of discomfort for trustees as well as the president;
as psychologist Harry Levinson points out, those in the position of
evaluating often have "the unconscious feeling that to appraise
someone negatively is to destroy him."[6] Levinson has observed that
this feeling interferes with rational decision making, particularly in
the area of performance appraisal.[7]

Perhaps recognizing some of the potential problems in performance
evaluation and attempting to avoid them, the president of Poe College
has requested an evaluation for himself but has coupled it with a self-
evaluation of the board, both to be incorporated in an upcoming

accreditation study. The board chairman describes how this plan came about:

> The president talked with me about this, and then he and I met with the executive secretary [of the accrediting association] at the president's house for breakfast. We thought the board ought to be evaluated, and the president would like an evaluation of himself. You know, Brewster asked for this too; they do it at Yale, and why can't we do it here [in Collegetown]?[8]
>
> It will be an interesting drill. We are at the beginning of a learning curve.

4 Board and President in Crisis: Case Studie

Perhaps because periodic formal evaluation of the president's overall performance does not have official standing on the board's agenda, problems involving the president come to the board room indirectly, often piecemeal, sometimes gathering momentum while trustees try to understand what is going on and what, if anything, they should do about it. If, as the issues and events unfold, the board reaches a point where its members are actively discussing whether or not to retain the incumbent president, one may think of the college as being in crisis. Among the ten colleges in this study, difficulties of crisis proportions were evident at two institutions. At Cummings College, the board had just completed an extensive performance review of the president which had consisted of interviews conducted by trustees on campus with faculty, students, and staff, and the board had decided to retain the president. At Faulkner College, difficulties between the president and the board resulted in the president's resignation and departure from campus in the middle of the academic year. In addition, at a third college, here referred to as Anonymous College to prevent identification of my informant by the president and members of the board, it seems likely that a crisis might occur if the two or three trustees hoping to engineer the president's departure cannot stage-manage events in the way they envision.

In none of these cases, interestingly, is the president's problem described as out-and-out administrative incompetence. What brings the issue of presidential performance to a head are the intangibles of presidential leadership, so that at Cummings the problem is phrased as a "question of whether the president is the right person to lead the college." Such abstractions are not easily discussed by trustees with the president. It is difficult, even embarrassing, to talk face-to-face with a man or woman about the kinds of behavior, often nuances, that are producing negative reactions among others, and the board-president relationship, with its paradoxical expectation that the board both support and evaluate the president, presumably makes these conversations even more difficult than if there were an unambiguous superior-subordinate relationship. As a result, in the absence of any clear signal to change, a president's behavior patterns are likely to persist and to be acknowledged only in the gossip of trustees, faculty, and others who are in a position to observe.

Although the particular ways in which relationships between board and president will go awry are unique to each situation, certain weaknesses within the governing board itself can endanger a healthy and productive association, and the three case studies included here illustrate these characteristic vulnerabilities. One such weakness, exemplified at Faulkner College, is the capacity of the board to be carried along by a very small group which is vocal about its objective and persistent in trying to achieve it. How such a small group may form is illustrated in the section on Anonymous College, where a concerned trustee questions the effectiveness not only of the president but of the governing board as well.

Another weakness, illustrated by Cummings College, is the board's capacity as a decision-making body to absorb informally a significant level of complaints about the president before feeling prompted to place those complaints on the formal agenda. By delaying, a board may appear to others to be putting its collective head in the sand at worst, or equivocating at best. In either case, the result may be that the board misses the moment when it could most constructively intervene. Under other circumstances, however, delay may be a positive response, a demonstration that the board is relatively immune to the professional complainers and idle gossip that characterize any organization.

Performance Review at Cummings College

Cummings College is situated on a seventy-two-acre campus about ten minutes' walk from the town square. The board of trustees has thirty-five members, all but two of whom are graduates of the college, with many representative of the corporate, educational, and legal elite of various major metropolitan areas across the nation. About one-third of the board members live within an hour's drive of the campus; some of the others, when in town for their four yearly meetings, stay with faculty friends who live on the quiet residential streets adjacent to the campus.

The president of Cummings for the past seven years has been Dr. Daniel Allbritten, an archeologist whose scholarly interests have focused on Central and South America. Reflecting on the process he has undergone in developing a relationship with the board, President Allbritten invokes a metaphor of sculpting, "It's like taking clay and working on its shape." He also describes trustees as "guides" and speaks of presenting projects in their "early development" to board members, and to the faculty as well, and of "tak[ing] my orientation from their responses." Dr. Allbritten has observed a great deal of informal interchange at Cummings between the students and faculty and the board members. Although in principle he does not object to this dynamic, he draws a word picture of students and faculty "collar[ing]" trustees as they walk across the campus, a practice he feels draws trustees too much into everyday problems and sometimes inclines the board to take on the role of a "problem-solving senate."

In the opinion of Cummings board members, the president finds most worrisome the relationships between individual faculty members and individual trustees. During weekend board meetings, some trustees spend many evening hours in the faculty lounge before going to a faculty home for the night. The chairman of the board, retired from his professorship at an Ivy League university, apparently disapproves of these informal, even intimate conversations, but he only remarks, "A different kind of board chairman might get involved [in those conversations], but I have felt the chairman ought to stay a little clear of that." Still, as he observes, "Some board members love to gossip with the faculty," and it was through those conversations, he says, that the board perceived that "the faculty was unhappy [about the president]. We picked up static from some faculty. There was enough smoke that we thought we ought to see if there was a real fire."

During this period the president was achieving excellent results according to what one board member calls the "usual criteria: fund raising, admissions, and so on." Even so, there were some trustees, especially committee chairmen who worked closely with the president, who were antagonized by his personal manner; they began to say that the president was "negative and thin-skinned." Although complaints by faculty members centered on the president's personal manner, his problems with them were not entirely ones of style. Apparently, according to one well-informed trustee, when Dr. Allbritten first took office he did not realize the extent to which the faculty, under his predecessors, had established itself as predominant over the administration. Unaware of "this tension on the campus for which he would be held accountable," the president appointed three faculty advisory committees to make recommendations on three issues: the elimination of an academic department, the selection of a chairman for another department, and the status of the faculty-student ratio. On the Cummings campus, such faculty advisory committees "always think they're decision-makers," and whatever hard feelings were caused by the president's personal manner were increased when he did not follow their advice. They "thought he was being dictatorial," says another trustee, when much of what he was doing was "rechanneling" resources. Cognizant of these factors, this trustee was persuaded that the president had a significant problem only after being personally approached by a highly respected faculty member, just retired, who "felt he was protecting the future of the college in talking to me about this."

The manner in which these faculty criticisms were transformed into a trustee committee to review the administration occurred "obliquely" according to one board member, who theorizes vaguely that "maybe there was pressure put on the chairman to organize a review," pressure presumably exerted by the board members identified as "carpers." Another trustee, a committee chairman, recalls the ambiguity that surrounded the initial conversations in the board room as the results of the complaints about the president began to surface there:

> The chairman made a series of statements over several meetings: we want to look at the president and the board. And then it evolved over several meetings, and I remember [the board chairman] saying these things. I didn't know anything more.

The decision-making process on this issue was sufficiently fragmented and private that, when asked to describe what events crystallized the idea that there ought to be some sort of formal review of the president, this trustee replied, "I don't know," and continued:

> There are two stories. Number one that Dan [the president] started it. The Brewster example was held up as the progressive thing to do, and Dan expected a strong show of support.[1] Number two is that people on the board were quite unhappy, and this was a way to pacify them.
> My guess is it was both.

During these early discussions, which took place during the president's fifth year in office, the board talked in its meetings about "do we want to go ahead, what are the dangers," with the lead role taken by the chairman who, according to one trustee, "thought the president was doing a fine job and thought that people would be taking pot shots through an administrative review." And to be sure, the chairman did feel ambivalent:

> There was a lot of discontent with the way the president was handling things. Then there's the question, what do you do about it? I understood

Dan's situation. I was [once] chairman of a physics department, and I wondered how I could know if I was doing a good job.

As the process continued to unfold, the board chairman eventually felt agreement had been reached supporting the concept of an "administrative review." This particular nomenclature, which was to be distinguished from an evaluation of the president, was intended to suggest to the campus that a rather impersonal review of the upper administrative echelon was to take place, but this "thinly disguised substitute" had little effect, and it was well recognized that the president was on trial. In the meantime, the president had told the board that if the review were to take place promptly, which would be during April and May, he could not survive it, his position on campus at the end of the academic year not being strong enough to withstand the scrutiny of what was apparently to be a public pro-ceeding. For this reason the review was delayed, and an ad hoc committee was appointed by the chairman to work with the president in deciding upon a plan.

The appointment of the appropriate people to the ad hoc committee was a matter of grave concern to the chairman, who recalls, "We needed a committee which was astute, sensitive, intelligent, discreet, and we were fortunate to have that kind of people on the board." Others interviewed do not wholly agree with this assessment, noting that qualities of discretion and sensitivity are not necessarily associated with good boardsmanship at Cummings, where the trustees pride themselves on operating in a climate of openness. It is likely that other factors weighed heavily with the chairman, and one who was appointed to the committee speculates that the selection was "probably made in consultation with the president, going for people who could meet with some frequency, who had some credibility, and [who had] balancing points of view." In an unusual move, the chairman asked the committee to "write its own charge." The president, said to have been "dismayed" by this development, presumably wondered about his own position if the committee were to pursue a course that did not meet with the approval of the board as a whole.

The five committee members included two professional women, one of them an educational administrator who describes herself as typically "starting out on the liberal wing but really listening" and winding up in a more moderate position, a nationally known educator, the chairman of the board, and a trustee in his eighties reported to have been equal to his share of the work and more. A sixth trustee, a retired banker living relatively near the campus, was asked to collate all the materials and make a report to the president.

Over a period of several months, the ad hoc committee met ten times for two hours each session, and according to two trustee participants, the time was "not wasted." The president, having been "in on it from the beginning," met with the committee to discuss "process," the committee not wishing to undertake "anything that the president would disagree with procedurally." The committee also met and "checked" with the faculty's committee on faculty procedures and met as well with past presidents of the student government. Although the board had tentatively planned its own self-study to be concurrent with the administrative review, the ad hoc committee concluded that both reviews running simultaneously would be more than the board could handle, and the self-study was postponed until after the administrative review had been completed. As time went on, the ad hoc committee evolved into the group that was actually going to carry out the review, although one member says she cannot recall when, or by what process, the committee members became the "hit guys."

The committee decided to interview selected faculty, administrators, students, and a few alumni, and it sent out a public letter that one trustee recalls as "technically worded" in an attempt to take the onus off the president:

> [It said something like] we are going to do an evaluation of the president and the president's staff with respect to how they relate among themselves and with other constituencies of the college.
>
> We told all that we were glad to hear from them by letter and that we would be seeking out certain members of the faculty and administration. We said we would be glad to hear anything and would guarantee them anonymity.

The committee members were uncertain about their approach, wondering "Have we opened a can of worms that we can't put the lid back on?" and feeling that "the credibility of the board depended on how we comported ourselves." They spent nearly two weeks on campus interviewing 160 people, "anybody who wanted to meet with us, and others in whom we were interested." Two trustees sat in on each interview, in which the interviewee was asked to respond to a "standard set" of questions especially developed to guide the conversations.

Interviews with members of the ad hoc committee several months after the review was completed revealed a disparity of feeling as they looked back on the process. One member had begun the review thinking that discontent was localized within the junior faculty but found it was widespread in the senior faculty as well. She recalls thinking, "I believe in the process and this is what we are finding out," and she also recalls being "impressed with the candor [of the people on campus] and by the trust they were putting in us." While this trustee characterized the interviews as "wide-open," another was struck by "how difficult [it is] to find out what people think":

> We really had to dig to find out what the administration was thinking. I remember one who refused to talk. We called on his loyalty: you've got to come [and talk to us]. We almost had to subpoena him.
>   It's difficult to get much from the administration . . . and you have to take the faculty with a grain of salt.

In conducting the interviews, the trustees faced the problem of trying "to be sympathetic and yet not give the impression that we agreed with what they were saying." The review was a public process, a report was to be issued, and the trustees in a sense would be held accountable for the responses they had given during the interviews.

A problem that disturbed the trustee assigned to convey the results of the review to the president was the question, "Can style be assessed?" How, in practice, can trustees measure the positive or negative impact of the "tone" of a president's behavior? How could the trustees of Cummings College determine if, or how, the welfare of the college was negatively affected by a personal manner that was perceived as "arrogant and thin-skinned"? These qualities are difficult to discuss without seeming to stray into mere gossip, and one trustee reported with relief and some pride that discussion in the board room concerning the ad hoc committee's findings remained at a dignified level: "It was an impressive meeting, with everyone trying to become genuinely informed, avoiding the temptation to get gossipy. But it did lay out the problems."

The board had to decide whether to fire the president or "give [him] a chance to regroup," says one trustee, and it was "a tough decision for thirty-five people to make," says another. In the chairman's view, "It could have wound up that we got rid of [him]," but a spirit of tolerance and practicality prevailed, as this board member reveals: "It was courageous of the board to keep him. Of course, we were early in a fund-raising campaign. . . . [But we said,] let's give the guy a chance. Things aren't that bad." The report of the board to the campus was brief and formal, confined, as one trustee paraphrased it, to the statement, "We're convinced that there are some real problems, but the president is perfectly capable of running things with our help."

When the report came out, there was "a lot of unhappiness" on the part of certain faculty members and students who had assumed the president would be "fired." Some were outraged—"After what I told them, they didn't fire him?"—but, as the board chairman observed philosophically, "You expect some of this." Disappointment in the report may also have been exacerbated by the expectation, voiced when the review was first announced, of a "whitewash," and the board's short statement supportive of the president did very little to assuage those feelings. In reflecting upon these reactions, which apparently were not in the majority, a member of the ad hoc committee recalls that the committee took a rather hard-boiled attitude: "The committee couldn't have cared less how [the report] was received. We did what we had to do, and [if they consider it a whitewash], that's their problem." This trustee goes on to say that the opinion actually prevailing on campus was more positive—and more sophisticated: "Most of the people felt that what went on behind the scenes with the trustees and the president was what was important," while the report itself was not so significant.

When the president was confronted with the details of the negative findings that lay behind the board's brief formal report, his reaction apparently was extraordinarily open and positive: "Well, if that's what they're saying, we'll have to make some changes." In this difficult situation, according to the trustee who spoke privately with Dr. Allbritten to deliver the committee's findings, "the president showed what he was really made of, and he does have wonderful qualities." Another trustee observes that there was "critical and hard talking" with the president, and since then there have been "some real changes."

Cummings trustees say in retrospect that if the board "had been doing our job," it would have known what was going on and perhaps the review would not, as the chairman puts it, have had to be so "drastic." To help prevent a similar crisis from arising in the future, two or three specific changes have been made in the way the board communicates with the president about his performance. First, to enhance ongoing communication, the chairman and vice-chairman of the board meet with the president one evening each month, for a "hair-down" discussion in which the president can "talk over policy and decision making." In the past, these discussions had taken place between the chairman and the president, and the chairman finds having a third person present "very helpful." However, another member of the board familiar with this arrangement says it is difficult for the chairman and vice-chairman to provide support to the president and simultaneously deliver objective, and of necessity sometimes negative, evaluations and advice. This trustee suggests that "if you have to give support and then criticize, maybe you need a committee structure behind you; otherwise, it comes down to personalities." Perhaps it was this same trustee who, in a subsequent self-study by the board, recommended anonymously that a Committee on the President, or a Committee on the Administration, be developed with "specific responsibility for keeping in touch with the president personally and his role . . . and [for] present[ing] critiques when necessary." Another trustee wonders if the informal "information systems" of the chairman and vice-chairman will always be a good index of campus and board sentiment. But for the immediate future, since a "base line" of data was developed during the administrative review, this trustee believes that critiques of the president, by whomever conducted, can be reasonably accurate and explicit.

A second outcome of the review was authorization of the chairman, the vice-chairman, and the trustee who chaired the ad hoc committee to undertake an annual review of the president's performance and to convey their findings to the Executive Committee. This review is to be "informal" and will not go to the full board because "an executive session of the whole board would signal the community that some big deal was going on." But the chairman stresses that there is value and importance in this new procedure because it will be "automatic and annual."

Contemplating these new arrangements, which place a considerable burden of responsibility on board members to develop informants and, if necessary, to interpret the campus mood for the president, one trustee argues that having good sources of information is among a college president's responsibilities. He suggests that a president should cultivate one or two informants on campus to whom he makes it clear that he "wants to know the truth even if it hurts a little."

When Cummings trustees were asked about the results overall of a public presidential review, the only positive outcome mentioned by the board chairman was its public relations effect, whereby people on campus "got the feeling that the board is willing to listen." Otherwise, his views are negative: "There's an inherent danger in stirring things up. I hope never to go through it again. It's probably the board's most difficult endeavor."

Others were much more positive. One feels "pretty strongly . . . that the president benefited enormously and would not have survived without it." She points out that this review was undertaken because the board was fairly certain "there were some things [the president] had to hear" and the board "needed evidence" to formulate its conversation with him. This trustee concludes that "maybe we stirred up more waves than necessary . . . [but] most of the process was healthy." When I asked if her favorable opinion of the review process would have been affected had the president not been so cooperative in trying to make appropriate changes, she replied that her opinion would have depended upon whether the president had resigned and how difficult the board would have found the transition to a new administration.

Most arresting in the reactions of board members is the implication that the impact of the review on relationships within the board is as important to them as its impact on the president and the campus constituencies. Perhaps my questions elicited this somewhat self-absorbed response, but the substance of the interviews supports the interpretation that the Cummings board narrowly escaped firing the president in the course of dealing with divisiveness within its own ranks. Though no trustee said so directly, there is the suggestion that the board was seriously divided before the review and unified afterward: "The carpers really did shut up for a while. It brought the board back together." Another trustee, the one who remarked that the review gave the president the opportunity "to show what he was really made of," expressed similar feelings about the board, as if crisis brought forth the group's best qualities: "I wouldn't change anything [about the review process]. We didn't do anything negative; we wanted the truth and had no preconceived ideas. It was wonderful."

The review process at Cummings, it appears, forced board members to talk among themselves and to think about their role and about the welfare of the college in very specific terms. This had a unifying effect as the findings of the ad hoc committee progressed through the decision-making structure:

> The ad hoc committee and the Executive Committee and the board all went through parallel processes. People felt good about it. There was genuine consensus that this is the right thing to do. . . . We were quite together.

* * * * *

In contrast to Cummings College where faculty complaints were important in rousing the board to action, at Faulkner College, in the case study that follows, the faculty and students play little or no part in forcing the question of the president's performance onto the board's agenda. In the Faulkner case, the recruitment of the president is clouded by lack of communication, and the personal motives of the trustee cabal that forms to remove him are problematic, as is the shrewdness of a president whose actions seem to invite, rather than to deflect, further complications. All of these problems are aggravated as much by widespread resentment of the president's wife as by the unwieldly structure of the governing board.

Dismissing the President at Faulkner College

Faulkner College occupies sixty acres along a stream near the center of a town of 15,000. Its board is unusually large, with over fifty members, 90 percent of them alumni. Six trustees live in the college town, and several others have established summer residences in a nearby lakefront development. The board's membership is representative of the achieved success of many Faulkner graduates, and one trustee characterizes the group by saying, "Just take a dart board and throw darts at a list of Faulkner alumni."

Hugh Piers Zeleny was selected for the presidency of Faulkner College at a time when, according to one member of the board, "[He] was a leading candidate in the country. He looked awfully good on paper—and he was." Zeleny, then approaching forty, had been educated at one of New England's elite men's colleges and afterward had earned both a law degree and a doctorate in philosophy. When approached by Faulkner, he was academic dean at a respected liberal arts college and had "turned down previous presidential assaults":

> But I had to get it out of my system. And the job at Faulkner was unusual: non-fund-raising and non-P.R. . . .
>
> My job as president over five to eight years was [to be] a job of administration. People needed to be fired. There was a troubled chief financial officer, [outside business deals involving] the vice-president for public relations and members of the board. And there were a bunch of other concerns, some of which in my view [the board members] were wrong about.
>
> There was also an enormous deficit. They needed a strong administrator and strong leader but someone who could also lead the faculty. For them and for me I seemed like the perfect match, and [with my Ph.D. and college teaching background] I could even give the faculty their bone. I had a lot of image when I came.

In the minds of some of the governing board, however, the search had been carried out too fast, and it did not weigh with them that Zeleny might have been recruited by another college if the Search Committee had not quickly made him an offer. In addition, the chairman of the Search Committee had consciously tried to keep the details of the search very private in an attempt to protect the reputations of candidates who were not chosen. He recalls:

> We made a mistake in not exposing the candidate, but I was shocked by the conduct of most search committees and tried to keep things confi-

dential. I did not want to put the candidates up for election [by the board]. So the board took Zeleny on our say-so, but people felt they hadn't had their say, and they wondered, "Who is he, anyway?"

Another circumstance, which seemed "weird" to Zeleny, was that he was "never in contact with faculty and students until the decision was made":

Two weeks before I came to the campus [to meet faculty and students], the head of the Search Committee said, "You're the one, but they can veto you—but you're the only one they're going to meet." So I met with half a dozen faculty in a group meeting and a half a dozen students in a group meeting.

A trustee not on the Search Committee also recalls there was very little consultation about the candidate and the job to be done:

When Zeleny was selected, I'm not sure there was a common under-standing of what he would do and there were lots of assumptions. He was largely selected by a search committee which didn't communicate their assignment to the president to the board and the rest of the residential community. So you start with a recipe for trouble.

When he assumed office, Zeleny turned his attention to adminis-trative problems: admissions, about which he thought Faulkner "too complacent," and the necessity of "hav[ing] to fire deans during the first year." He also recalls thinking that although he "didn't understand the structure" of the governing board, "I didn't have to pay much attention." And to be sure, the structure of the Faulkner board is unusual in that the Executive Committee of twelve trustees, which meets five or six times each year, is presided over by the *vice*-chairman of the board, while the chairman of the board, who does not sit on the Executive Committee, presides only at semiannual meetings of the full board. It is an arrangement, according to the chairman, that results in a "leadership vacuum":

You don't have a focal point that you can go to with complaints. No one considers himself the chief person and is willing to take up questions. I'm certainly not disinterested, but [as chairman], I don't have the au-thority, and I'm reluctant myself.

And then the chairman adds, "But a strong president will fill the gaps and run the college the way he wants to."
Concern about leadership is also expressed by the vice-chairman

of the board, a retired lawyer. As he looks back on the tenure of Dr. Zeleny, he muses, "I'm supposed to be somewhat of a leader, but I don't know if I've led." And he observes, "[With the previous president], I used to talk a good deal, but I've done this to a lesser extent with Zeleny. And I'm afraid he didn't talk to enough people about what he was doing." The vice-chairman goes on to recall with evident pleasure the prior administration, when he occasionally spent the night in the president's house and had breakfast the next morning with the former president, a bachelor, and he remarks, "There was a lot more informality then, without a wife and children" in the house.

Another trustee, a professor in a graduate professional school, has observed that the Faulkner president typically has relatively little contact with the board as a whole but usually works closely with the Executive Committee:

> But Zeleny was confident and tended not to rely on the Executive Committee and viewed their role as ratification of administrative decisions.
>
> [However], such a small and stable group begins to believe they will always be very influential with the president. These were expectations that he had no reason to know [nor was there any reason to expect] that he would be advised of these matters.
>
> A small group with this history needed to be consulted. Zeleny's problems were a result of structure and people.

These were not the structural and interpersonal problems that Zeleny recognized, however. What he found "almost incredible [was] that the board would not drive itself to consensus" but appeared accustomed to proceed on the basis of majority votes. He found that the committee meetings included representatives of the faculty and students and sometimes the alumni and were consequently so large that they "were almost always public sessions—the ability to have a private, quiet conversation was practically zero." He also found the committee system "extraordinarily confused" and discovered that the same member might vote differently on an issue as it moved from committee to committee, so that "as president, you have to be prepared to fight the battle anew with each layer."

Even so, it was Zeleny's view up through the spring of his second year in office that there was no cause for alarm in his relationship with the board:

> Until last spring, the governing board was not high on my list of priorities to solve. I thought the board was not easy, but workable. Then a group of them tried to get me thrown out.

That spring I had mentioned a conflict of interest to one trustee and a vice-president for public relations who are involved [together] in real estate and maybe more. I had heard gossip and I went to the vice-president and said it ought to be reported as a conflict of interest [in our annual report]. But the vice-president said, "It's not serious," and I dropped the subject. And then I was told there was substance to it. I'm one for principle: I said, "We do have the form and it ought to be filled out," and we agreed that next year it would be reported. . . .

I sensed that the vice-president was upset, and I knew that the trustee [Ed Fraser, a member of the Executive Committee] was furious . . . but obviously, I was on more than secure ground.

At the [time of the] April meeting of the Executive Committee, Fraser and two of his buddies on the Executive Committee laid me out, and they were accompanied by the [then] chairman and the vice-chairman as onlookers. I arranged the dinner at my house, and they really laid into me: number one, the coeducation of fraternities [which I supported] deeply violated tradition; number two, the Committee on Investments in South Africa was Socialist, if not Communist; three, the Women's Commission on campus was fomenting trouble.

And then one of his buddies attacked my wife, said nobody liked her and she wasn't friendly.

I asked if anyone had had too much to drink.

Yes, two out of the three of them were smashed, but they were in the President's House, and there was no way for Helen to miss it. I said to myself, he's drunk and maybe it'll go away.

I asked if the chairman and vice-chairman had spoken up during this meeting.

I can't get angry with the vice-chairman because he didn't say it was beyond the pale. He talks in parables, in circumlocutions, and he would tell a story. And my response was to do nothing. The bigger the crisis, the quieter I get.

Helen and I lay awake all night. She didn't feel that I should just hand in my resignation. But I knew Fraser had four weeks between then and the full board meeting in May and that he would be trying to get me out of office.

And he thought he had the votes. There were a couple of meetings without my attendance but [one of his two buddies at the dinner meeting] jumped off, as practically everybody else did, and there was nobody of any significance left in the dump-Zeleny movement.

And out of this came an Advisory Committee to give me advice on what the hell was going on. I had felt the need for this a long time ago, but the [former] chairman of the board had dragged his feet. So in this crisis, they formed an Advisory Committee to give advice and evaluate me and that was okay with me. And it worked for two meetings.

The current board chairman, who observed events from a city 150 miles away, recalls the spring and summer as a period when a small group of trustees was getting together unofficially before board meetings and perhaps meeting with the president and not necessarily representing the views of the whole board, but no one felt he had the authority to intervene. Apparently several of the cabal lived near the campus, and in the view of the chairman, "they knew too much, really," a judgment with which the vice-chairman appears to agree, based on his observations from his summer home on the nearby lakefront: "Certainly last summer there was too much [contact by trustees with the campus]. Why I was somewhat left out I don't know."

A third trustee, who observed events from a distance of several hundred miles, believes that when Edward Fraser became upset with the president, other members of the board could have said, "You're being silly," but instead felt they had to appoint a committee to oversee the president, an action that he feels assured the president's eventual resignation or dismissal:

> I don't know how many were aware when the [Advisory] Committee was formed that it meant the president would have to leave. Maybe four or five had that perception. . . .
>   If a board anticipates [events], then they eliminate the options a president might have. Being president of a small college is hard enough [without that]. . . . I would wait until things cracked [rather than taking anticipatory action].

The fourth trustee interviewed, new to the board and only several years a graduate, says "the Zeleny issue is so cloudy" that she is "not sure I understand the real details." She recalls:

> The Advisory Committee had information but never went into details with the board. I found very much of what they said to be vague and a lot not concrete. . . . [The idea was that] he just wasn't everything people wanted him to be. . . . He's not a person's person; [by that I mean] he couldn't mold himself to every situation. . . . When we looked at the long-range plan, he didn't fit.
>   A lot of time and work went into it. He was given six months to change and it didn't seem to work out. I thought it admirable that he knew what was going on. No one was stabbing him in the back or asking him to leave.

Zeleny is not a graduate [of Faulkner]. Is that important? . . . It may
well be. You have to have gone there and know what goes on.

Dr. Zeleny's recollection of the events of the spring and summer
is naturally more specific than that of the young trustee living in
another state, and he cites one particular event as "what did me in":

In the spring I chaired the [administration-faculty-student] committee
which handles student discipline. Two white guys had taken off their
pants and peed outside Afro-American House, so they were to be pun-
ished—it was not just wild oats. [So the committee decided] not to throw
them out of school, which leaves a permanent scar on their record, but
to assign them to the president, who would give them an independent,
noncredit study on prejudice.

I asked if it had been his idea that they be apprenticed to him for
this punishment because he has a Ph.D. in philosophy, and Dr. Zeleny
replied, "In part, yes."

But what did me in was that one of the boys was a grandson of a trustee
emeritus who is rich and went bananas, and that's all Fraser needed.
And the two of them had a good time, although by Commencement they
couldn't quite get the board enough in a stew [to fire me].
    Then Fraser announced his resignation from everything at Faulkner,
the Advisory Committee had one or two shots to make, and armed with
the rich grandfather, they had about six issues and these things accumulate. Then the board had to decide whether to face these six or twelve
issues and take the chance of the Advisory Committee members resigning, or tell me to leave.
    In August, some people started a whisper campaign against my wife.
. . . It's not clear where it started [but the gossip was] that she is not well
liked in town. Some people said, "I can't tell you who told me this but
you have a president whose wife didn't go to college." The thing is, she
has the appearance of a perfect president's wife. Our biggest problem is
that we look like a perfect little family. It's true my wife didn't go to
college, but here we are, this perfect nuclear family. . . .
    Well, that [rumor] really destroyed Helen because of its unfairness and
partly because a wife has no way to get back but sits there and takes the
punishment and watches me take it.
    I knew then it was all over. In September I met with the Advisory
Committee, and we agreed to call it off while we could still be civil.

One trustee did not believe Dr. Zeleny had done anything to merit
being fired, but he felt Zeleny had been so damaged by the attack
that his future effectiveness was impaired, "So you choose between

defending that individual and the good of the institution." And he continues:

> Between the president and the board there should be an informal mechanism [for communication]. There really has to be. There have to be avenues of communication between the president and those who have the greatest influence on the future of the college. If Zeleny had done this, there would have been no problem. . . .
>
> If I were president, I would soon—if I were smart—find seven or eight people that I ought to talk to from time to time. Then when you go to the board, you've tested the idea and gotten supported. . . .
>
> [What this amounts to is] just understanding what's out there, an ability to get a reading from those who have influence and knowledge. It's no different from the business world. I attend a lot of board meetings and most good CEOs test ideas. "Why don't you give me a call back in a couple of days," they'll say; they don't ask for an immediate decision. People who don't do that get in terrible trouble.

And he concludes:

> A college president gets in deep trouble by being isolated, and the formal structure of the governing board can be very isolating, notwithstanding all the meetings you have.

* * * * *

While prestigious institutions like Cummings and Faulkner can expect in future years to maintain their present highly competitive position in undergraduate admissions, and while Cummings's endowment of over $70 million is sufficient to weather substantial inflation, depression, and deficits, Anonymous College, in the selection that follows, is in a far more marginal position. Of the ten colleges included in this research, Anonymous is among the two or three with the greatest potential for trouble during the current reduction in the cohort of eighteen to twenty-five year olds. At present, the Anonymous board must choose among maintaining admissions standards, maintaining enrollment, or trying to do both by underwriting a major public relations campaign for which funds might have to be borrowed. There is a basis for urgency.

The president of Anonymous is much less naïve than Faulkner's Zeleny about the relationship between the board and the president, but like the president of Cummings, he has had a hard time "locating [his] style" with the board. He says that he should develop closer ties with trustees, but like some other presidents, he lacks the will or discipline or perhaps the time to pick up the telephone as frequently as, upon reflection, he feels he should. His instinctive wariness of the board seems at odds with an intellectual view that the board has no reason not to support him.

The way trustee feelings about the president's performance are handled at Anonymous—or to be more accurate, the way those opinions are not acknowledged—illustrates graphically the potential for disharmony on the board and the potential for opposition to the president that can be galvanized by one or two energetic trustees, especially in the absence of strong leadership by the chairman. One can see in Mr. Parson, a trustee whose views are transcribed below, the kind of determination that could not be handled by the Faulkner board and that played a large part in precipitating the president's forced resignation.

Trouble Brewing at Anonymous College

Joseph Langhorne Parson is a graduate of Anonymous College and was in school during the period when the college was headed by an autocratic president in the "heroic" mode. An executive by vocation and horseman by avocation, he is also involved in the affairs of the college's alumni association and might travel to the campus—a two-hour drive—once a month to confer with the alumni and development staffs. This familiarity with the inner workings of the administration, coupled with the opportunity to talk to two other alumni trustees working with him on the Anonymous Fund for Excellence, has brought to a head his criticisms of both the board and the president and has stimulated his plans for taking action. Here he speaks for himself in comments excerpted from a two-hour interview in the parlor of his nineteenth-century farmhouse:

> [Several years ago] I was asked to take over the chairmanship of the science center capital campaign. Such a position, I thought, should be on the board, and I told the Development Director that the position needed clout. I guess all this was negotiated at the college and three or four months later I was appointed to the board. . . .
>
> It's not a working board. A few of us are busting our tails while others put Anonymous College in the file until the next meeting. . . . Casual is the word for all aspects of the board. . . .
>
> The present chairman of the board backed into the job. No one else had the stature. It was to be for one year and is now two or three. . . .
>
> [The chairman] is not exerting leadership at all. To me he is not setting an example or instilling vigor in activating the board or taking more time to help the president. . . . [In my opinion], we need a different kind of chairman . . . someone with guts and enthusiasm and who is willing to work slowly and by observation through all problems. . . .
>
> [Our evaluation of the president is] pretty casual. We send him out of

the room for five minutes. This is in Executive Committee, it never comes to the full board. . . . At no time has there been a full board discussion [of the president's performance]. . . . [In Executive Committee] we have a schedule of items and the president's job and salary will be reviewed [according to the schedule]. . . .

When the president was brought up to be discussed, I said, "Well, guys, how do you feel?" But people are very ho hum. But I feel we need a stronger person. Since no one has suggested the timing for a change, I have requested a special Executive Committee meeting [to discuss this]. We know he's not great and have been saying that for two years and now he's been here seven years. The logical time for a change is ten years. Then if we can get that [time frame] out in the open, we can go about getting someone else.

My current feeling has picked up speed since the Fund for Excellence chairman came on the board and I heard his frustration over problems of communication on campus between offices. . . . Since then I have felt courage to make more overtures. Both of us are spreading out and talking to others, and we have two or three others who feel there needs to be change, but we haven't gone to those we don't know well. . . . There is a lot of blood to be shed.

Our president couldn't be a nicer guy, and it's somewhat of a personal disappointment to me to have to take this point of view about him.

The president and the college are accountable to us; we're holding the bag if it goes down the drain. Any other chairman would crack the whip, with or without the help of the president.

When I talk with the Executive Committee about the president, they will say, "We've been dying to do that for years." Then we will try to ease him out gracefully. It would take a great deal of discussion if we were to fire the president fast. In true form, Anonymous College will be conservative.

5 The Lonely Presidency

In the literature designed to educate trustees by describing how they should structure their relationship with the president, much is made of the board's role as a "sounding board" for the president and of the board's responsibility to "support" the president. In practice, however, it does not seem that a board can be as unfailingly supportive as the literature suggests and at the same time meet its responsibility to evaluate the president. Even when board members keep their disagreements with the president confidential to the board room—and not all do—there is an understandable tension basic to the relationship. For this reason, it is probably unrealistic to expect that the kind of help and understanding a board can give to a president will be a source of emotional support for him or her. Instead, most experienced college presidents distinguish between the "ideal" board, which supports the president, and their own board rooms where, as the president of Cather College remarks, "When things get tough, a few trustees always get bitchy."

The president of Faulkner College, realizing that his problems with the board were serious, made inquiries elsewhere in academia and was "struck by the number [of presidents] who are pushed out of their jobs." Perhaps this president exaggerates in suggesting that "most presidents are paranoid" about their boards, but it is a difference of degree between his overwrought view and the cooler assessment of the president of Frost College, who says of his contacts with board members, "Every day I'm evaluated." And his observation is correct, since most trustees, upon reflection, agree with the board member from Longfellow College who says, "At every meeting I'm reviewing [the president]—how he is handling student and faculty relations." In other words, making judgments about performance and competence is one aspect of virtually all trustee contacts with the president.

Keeping One's Distance

In this atmosphere, the reaction of many presidents is to keep their distance emotionally and to treat the board as one among the numerous constituencies with whom the president must deal. The president of Poe College, for example, identifies the board as one of fourteen constituencies but considers it sufficiently important that he "must know them as my family." He frequently "touches base" with members of his board by telephone and in this way tries to develop familial good feeling. Of course, some presidents, like the president of Longfellow, are not comfortable with breezy informality. Though he recognizes the value of personal ties—upon assuming the Long-fellow presidency three years ago, he traveled to visit with each trustee individually—he finds he does not "have the relationship" or the inclination to phone board members frequently to discuss issues informally. The president of Melville College says members of the board "have to be cultivated like major donors, or you just don't get good performance." But in practice, he admits, "keeping in touch is a problem." In fact, keeping in touch is such a widespread problem that it seems to be a kind of occupational hazard for presidents—the result of crowded schedules and, perhaps, some reluctance. Two presidents speak specifically of "neglecting" their boards. One is the president of Salinger College, who, after ten years in office, implies that trustees expect certain attentions from him, and he is concerned about short-changing them "in the allocation of my time, and I think some feel it." The president of another college, in office for a year and a half, has apparently not given much thought to his relationship with the board. He grew reflective as the interview progressed and began to speak of the utility—and pleasure—of "going to their homes and having them up here and taking them out on my boat." He continued to muse about the possible future value of an informal, friendly, and personal relationship with board members:

> When the chips are down, I may need their support. When I am doing things they don't agree with, they are not going to not disagree, but maybe they'll not let it go beyond disagreement.

Several presidents treat their boards with studied gingerness—they are kept "fully informed," says the Poe president; "no surprises" for the board, say the presidents of Longfellow and Frost. What these comments suggest is a special sensitivity on the part of presidents to the board's prerogatives, as those prerogatives are perceived by the board. For example, the president of Thoreau College describes a small real estate purchase about which several senior administrators "probably think they made the decision." Real estate, however, is a particular interest of the trustees, so before making a recommendation on the purchase, the president took care to check with members of the board "first, so I don't get burned."

Several presidents express significant feelings of alienation from their boards, none more poignantly than the president of Faulkner, who has discovered in the course of his presidency that they "just want a body; they don't want me." This president and the president of Cather seem to feel that not being an alumnus is a negative factor in relating to their boards. One speaks of himself as an "outsider" and "a real departure for Cather," while the other remarks that he "can't wrap himself in the Faulkner flag." Other presidents, even those who speak with the greatest sophistication about their boards, give signs of feeling estranged and defensive. "All they have to do is whisper, and I'm gone," says one, while another, in a wary and cynical moment, remarks:

> What they do is raise your standard of living, get you dependent on them, and then you slowly do just what they want you to do. When I came here, I settled lightly. I can find other things to do.

Two presidents have particularly interesting metaphors for describing how they keep their distance from the board and thereby protect themselves. The president of Poe College thinks of himself as an actor and of his relationship to the board as a performance; he closed our interview with this revelation: "If you're skillful, people forgive you because they enjoy the act. Always stop ten minutes early—and don't make the same mistake twice." The president of Frost views his relations with the board as a game in which he is not so much the high-stakes gamesman that Michael Maccoby made popular but rather the chief and most expert of the players.[1] He speaks of his board relationships variously as a "parliamentary game" and a "game of anticipation" in which "you have to constantly demonstrate that you know what's going on." In a comparison that may reflect his desire to establish himself with the trustees not merely as the chief, indispensable player but more potently as the omniscient referee, he tells the story of a fellow president who, unlike himself, is not a member of the governing board. He envies that president because "he can be a conscience, or watch them struggle with an issue and then come in from above like a god."

No One to Talk To

The presidents in this study say that they are isolated and think of themselves as lonely people. These feelings seem to exist for a variety of reasons. Perhaps a president stands apart as a reaction to pressure to appear superhuman or from a sense that aloofness goes hand in hand with the presidential position or from personal preference or from naïveté. Cut off from unrestrained fellowship with the trustees, "College presidents have no one to talk to," observes the president of Salinger, "and sometimes it shows, I'm afraid." The president of Frost thinks that the "education CEO" is more lonely than the "corporate CEO" because, in the business world, "you do your work in the daytime and then can be away; there are things you can feel finished with." In comparison, a college president's work stretches into the nighttime hours and the weekends, leaving less time for family and friends. Even the choice of friends is narrowed by exclusion of members of the administration and faculty, with whom most presidents feel they must maintain a certain social distance. The president of Frost, with over fifteen years of observation of his own and other presidents' circumstances, speaks with deep feelings of loneliness:

> I would never appoint a single man to be a president. You can't afford any special social friends [in the campus community]; a professional confidant is possible, but it's not healthy to keep secrets in the organization, and I don't think that does the job anyway. . . .
> Every president needs a good wife, and I have one!

II The Board as an Organizational Unit

6 The Board as a Volunteer Group

The ideal board would be nine [members] or smaller and everyone would need to be active and effective. Of course, this can't happen because trusteeship is not a paying proposition. —*Trustee, Frost College*

The activities of a board of trustees are greatly influenced by its status as a "volunteer group." That is, college trusteeship is an unpaid, leisure-time, and by implication, part-time activity of individuals who, over a year, may spend five to fifteen days on campus. Although the board of trustees is at the apex of the organization chart of any private college, it differs significantly from other elements of the college's structure. Unlike the administration and faculty, its services are not paid for, and its members have no formal role in the institution's day-to-day operations. Unlike students, board members are not paying clients of the institution. And unlike the alumni association, also a volunteer group, the board of trustees has a state-mandated relationship with the college. Given these characteristics, it may rightly be said that trusteeship consists of responsibility without material return, and we may legitimately wonder, first, what kinds of rewards motivate a trustee's participation and, second, how do these rewards affect the scope and character of the board's work?[1]

From the perspective of the board member, the place of college trusteeship in his or her life is akin to any volunteer activity that is said to contribute to the social good, except that trusteeship has a social status not usually associated with membership in a Kiwanis Club, Urban League chapter, or local P.T.A., although a similar status may be associated with membership on the board of a hospital or symphony. Since status is widely presumed to be an important factor in motivating individuals to join college boards, presidents and trustees alike quickly identify those who "like the honor" as distinguished from those who "want to contribute," and those trustees who do not make a contribution at least sufficient to offset the group's valuation of the honor of membership are viewed with opprobrium as "dead wood."

A trustee's contribution can come in a variety of forms, such as financial generosity, or a person's name can be a contribution in and of itself, as at Poe, where a well-known publisher is listed on the board roster and is said to be consulted by the president but "never" appears at board meetings. This kind of trustee, however valuable he or she may be to the college, is generally referred to as "inactive" in contrast to the "active" trustees interviewed for this study, almost all of whom are generous in their contribution of time—a commodity essential to the perpetuation of a volunteer group. These active trustees view time as a key element in board activity; they recognize that an individual volunteer's personal participation is fundamentally problematic, and they acknowledge this uncertainty by speaking of themselves as varying in "dedication." With time such an issue, it is not surprising to hear some presidents express relief that adequate attendance at regularly scheduled board meetings is not usually a problem, although arrangements for special additional meetings can be difficult. Overall, it seems to be the consensus of both trustees and presidents that, as one chairman remarked bluntly, "They do pretty well for a volunteer group."

Active trustees speak with good feeling of the rewards of "dedication" and seem to be candid in describing some of the incentives that prompt them to take leading roles. They speak of the opportunity for fellowship, whether conviviality pure and simple or the excitement of joint problem solving; of the need to fill time not otherwise so interestingly occupied; and of the desire to be associated with important persons, either out of personal preference or for the status conferred. Trustees also like to feel that they are "doing good" by supporting private colleges and the liberal arts tradition. The most important reward of all, however, appears to be the opportunity for self-development and the broadening of one's scope through exposure to new problems and challenges.

The Rewards of Trusteeship

Often trusteeship involves associating with people who are economically better off than oneself or professionally more accomplished or more socially prominent, associations that not only tend to increase status but also to enhance one's sense of self-worth. "It's fun to rub elbows with that crowd," remarks a trustee of Frost who, although an entrepreneur sufficiently successful to retire at fifty, admires those who have succeeded in the Fortune 500 environment. Similarly, a small city businessman on the Cather board values his contacts with big-time achievers, whether in education, investments, or the Fortune 500: "It's a pleasure to work intimately with these men; they're first-class people." In particular, it appears that the trustee who has risen high in the ranks of a Fortune 500 company has special cachet in the private college board room, as suggested by the president of Frost:

"They all come [to the board meeting] just because they want to be where [chief executive of a major corporation] is in attendance." Then too, for some younger trustees, appointment to a college board means not only glamorous new "contacts" but also another notch in the stick, another line in the résumé. "I was only thirty-two when they asked me," says a lawyer who clerked at the Supreme Court, and "I knew it couldn't hurt my image." "It was my first national board," says a forty-year-old Twain trustee who combines politics and academics, "and I was working with people who participate in running major institutions."

Other trustees mention a debt to the past. They attended college on scholarship and see in trusteeship the opportunity to make a kind of repayment:

> I owe Poe College something. I was on a scholastic scholarship, and I got a good education there. . . . My parents had both died, and I was lucky to have a chance to have a college education.

A Cummings trustee who became a department head at an Ivy League university is "grateful to the college" for the quality of education he received and still tells with relish the story of earning his Harvard doctorate in physics in fifteen months on the strength of his undergraduate preparation.

A recurring theme in conversations with trustees is the opportunity for self-development. This notion is described at some length by a Poe trustee, a small-city lawyer in his early thirties, who has obviously given the subject considerable thought:

> Young professionals begin to define their entire world view as bounded by the walls of their office. They begin to have many mercenary concerns. I feel depressed watching friends of my own suffering early middle age with no life outside their profession. Being on the board is an opportunity to deal in areas I don't deal in in my professional life.

Similar feelings are voiced by trustees twenty and thirty years older, who describe their work for the college as a "diversion," "a chance to have an avocation," and a relief from the frustrations of their careers:

> I had to think long and hard before I accepted [the chairmanship of the board]. I debated the effort [required], but it's another interest in life, different from running [a chemical] company.

Several trustees speak of college trusteeship as a way of "understanding" or keeping up with children who are of college age. Still others who are now retired speak of "hav[ing] the time to give" and of "want[ing] to keep my hand in with people who are doing things" in order to remain in the mainstream of life.

Fellowship, in the sense of teamwork to achieve a goal, is another reward of trusteeship, and members speak of themselves as being the kinds of people who "[have a] desire to participate and don't like to spectate." They say they "like to be involved," and a few give the impression that when trustees' interest is genuinely piqued by a project, the esprit de corps of the group can be very marked indeed, a kind of euphoria; members of the Investment Committee at Twain give this impression, as does the Executive Committee at Frost. Many trustees also speak of admiring members of the senior staff and of enjoying opportunities to work with them. Trustees describe these board-staff relationships as collegial, but the staff member is in a subordinate position and may feel an obligation to cultivate the board members' good will.

Another kind of fellowship, the "social aspect" as one Twain trustee puts it, involves spouses and the opportunity to include them in activities such as dinners, sports events, and occasionally certain presentations. At Twain, where the esprit de corps seems to be at a high level, one trustee describes weekend meetings at the college as equivalent in social homogeneity and conviviality to socializing in an elite New York City club. Similar feelings of social homogeneity exist at Salinger College; trustees are described as congenial "good old boys" for whom board meetings are an opportunity to "come back and see their friends." Among other trustees, particularly the trustees of Cather and Cummings, there is a sense of generalized affection for the school itself, and they say "it's nice to be back" and they "enjoy being there."

Sheer altruism also plays a part in motivating many trustees. One trustee "admires good things" and likes to have a hand in perpetuating them; another speaks of his role as a "public contribution," while another says that he "feel[s] a challenge in serving an institution free of government." Two other trustees, both senior officers in Fortune 500 companies, say their altruism has been nurtured by their corporations. One mentions that the founder of his company, to whom he was an assistant many years ago, was himself chairman of a college board and encouraged his young protégé's interest in alumni work. Another says his association with a college of which he is not a graduate "is directly related to [a] corporate policy" that encourages executives to contribute time and effort to various institutions in the communities where his company has plants and subsidiaries.

Naturally, members of a board do not respond uniformly to the rewards of trusteeship, and there is a wide variation among trustees in the amount of time devoted by the most and least active to board affairs. Of the one-third of board members who carry the burden of the work, many, including the chairmen, say they average one-and-a-half days of activity per month in addition to stated meetings. This total includes travel, telephone conferences, and committee meetings—"any time," as a trustee of Poe says, "that I can't make other appointments." At this level of commitment, a board member may become acutely conscious that personal and professional priorities limit the amount of time devoted to the college, and many mention with regret the meetings they have not attended because of business conflicts: "I don't do nearly enough," says the chairman of Cather, but "I don't have the time." In contrast, the participation of less active members may be limited to attendance at the three or four stated meetings per year, while others rarely attend at all.

Time as a Constraint

Although time is a constraint on any activity, whether professional, familial, or volunteer, it is also true that the clock often ticks perceptibly while college trustees pursue their activities, as suggested by this description of the formal board meeting at Salinger College, which takes place four times each year on a Saturday morning:

> The actual board meetings are perfunctory: they're set, sealed, and delivered. You can be sure if anyone makes a comment it's a grandstand play to be recorded in the minutes. . . .
> People come in from Boston, New York, and California, and everything is capsuled into one three-hour meeting, and if we do fall into a fruitful discussion, people are looking at their watches.

Indeed, board meetings that run past noon on Saturday risk inconveniencing not only those who want to attend a campus event, such as a football game, but also other, often less "dedicated" trustees who are eager to be on their way home from a sometimes rather inaccessible college town.

Some trustees try to make double use of their time devoted to the college, as does one very active Twain trustee in New York City who arranges as many college meetings as possible over lunch. Then too, volunteer priorities may change; this has apparently happened with a board chairman who has recently been spending less time on the college, where things appear to be going well, and proportionately more time on the struggling artists' society of which he is patron.

What the press of time upon trustee affairs obviously suggests is that the rewards of trusteeship are not sufficient to offset the benefits of participating in other activities of home, friends, and profession—nor would anyone involved expect them to be. Furthermore, the description by active trustees of their own high levels of interest and participation can be misleading, if not leavened by comments such as this one by a former college president, a trustee of Cummings, who remarks that "most board members do not expect to think about college affairs between meetings." And, in much the same vein, trustees at two other colleges observe that not all members present have read the materials mailed to them in advance of the meeting.

The question of how the rewards of trusteeship might be enhanced to stimulate further interest in the board was mentioned by three of the board chairmen. The chairman at Twain, for example, wants to involve spouses in more board activities, obviously hoping to build upon that board's already high social esprit de corps. Another chairman speaks of arranging board activities so that members "enjoy the meetings," while a third speaks of his role in pacifying any trustee "whose nose is out of joint," a circumstance that presumably occurs when the reward system breaks down. But on the whole, the burden of what social scientists call "group maintenance"—the provision of various kinds of rewards or benefits to those who participate in the group's activities—falls by default on the president.

The President as Executive Director of the Board

Although most college presidents are familiar with the dynamics of volunteer groups through their own participation in professional and community organizations, it is interesting that only one in this study seems to think of his own role vis-à-vis the board as similar to that of the executive director of a volunteer organization. Thus, while the president of Poe speaks of knowing the trustees as he "knows [his] family" and the president of Melville speaks of "cultivating the board as you would a major donor," it is only the president of Frost who speaks specifically of what he perceives as his own considerable leverage to withhold and confer benefits and his power to encourage individual participation and shape the board's thinking. Like other presidents, he recognizes that this leverage consists in part of personal attentions, whether they be a telephone call to ask advice, a breakfast tête-à-tête, or a hint to the chairman about a member who covets a particular committee chairmanship. And like many other presidents, the Frost president operates on the principle of "full disclosure," his cardinal rule being "no surprises"—surprise carrying with it the risk that board members might become alarmed and react in ways he considers undesirable. But more than the other president interviewed, this president seems consciously to try to anticipate trustees' reactions and to be willing to take specific steps to shape their reactions through explanation, persuasion, and information. For example, he describes arranging to be appointed to a national task force on academic excellence because he knows that neither his personal influence by itself nor the task force report by itself would be sufficient to bring the board to a point of view he thinks important to the future welfare of the college, whereas placing his influence in the context of a national report will be, he imagines, very persuasive.

Yet, regardless of the quality of the relationship a president may establish with the governing board, most find that trustee affairs are very time consuming. The president of Frost, for example, estimates that "literally 20 percent" of his time is devoted to matters directly or indirectly related to the trustees. Other presidents, with the exception of the president of Poe, who says that only 5 percent of his time is allocated to board activity, say they are reluctant to guess but mention 25 percent as the amount of time that intuitively seems accurate. These estimates are substantially higher than the 8 percent of time reported by Cohen and March in their study of presidential leadership,[2] a discrepancy probably resulting from the methodologies used. Cohen and March's statistic is based on an analysis of secretarial logs, whereas the informal guesses offered by the presidents in this study include collateral activities which may not be easily identified on a calendar, such as board-related visits with donors, staff meetings in which background papers for the board are planned or reviewed, and the cultivation of potential candidates for board membership.

The Committee Syste
and Key Trustees

It's important that every member bring
ent, experience, a desire to do somethir
for the college, and a willingness to woi
. . . Some members have never said a
word—I wouldn't know if they have a
thought in their heads.
Chairman of the Board, Longfellow College

The number of standing committees on the governing board varies
from college to college, with a minimum of three at Frost to as many
as fifteen at Faulkner. The average number of committees is eight,
each committee typically having three to five trustee members. Since
trustees have limited time available for college affairs, most boards
utilize their committees and build upon the opportunities they offer
for specialization of trustee interests and expertise and consequent
saving of time. This *modus operandi* predisposes the board to take on
the role of a panel of experts in which most members focus their
attention on one or perhaps two committee areas.

The Role of Committees

In the opinion of trustees, the most important of the board's
committees are finance, investments, and development, an indication
that the traditional areas of trustee interest—budgeting, managing
the endowment, and fund raising—continue to dominate the trustee
landscape. These are also areas in which trustees have customarily
made decisions without consulting with faculty and students—the
protests against investment in companies with holdings in South
Africa being a recent development whose outcome is, as yet, moot.[1]
With this exception, private college trustees have operated relatively
without constraint in matters of financial policy. For example, the
trustees at Frost speak of developing new guidelines for the management of the college portfolio; the trustees at Salinger shave a half a
percent off proposed salary increases in the course of a single meeting;
and the Cather trustees debate among themselves about whether to
borrow to build or to raise the funds first.

However, trustees' attitudes and the committee's role are quite
different in the area of educational policy, where trustees feel less
powerful. This committee tends to follow the faculty lead by passing
on to the board, usually unchanged, whatever recommendations the
faculty makes, as described by this Cummings trustee: "The stuff

that comes through [to the Academic Affairs Committee] has worked through the faculty, and we can't do very much about it when it comes to us." This faint feeling of helplessness combines with the lay board's conventional respect for the professional staff to assure that most faculty recommendations are simply ratified by the board.

In the area of student affairs, trustees are less passive, although there appears to be an unspoken wariness about the student potential for staging public protests. Indeed, this committee, while not typically activist, has in the last ten to fifteen years been the focus periodically of intense feeling both within the board and among students when curfews, visiting arrangements between the sexes, and coed dorms have been on the agenda. Similarly, a developing interest by trustees in issues such as the role of fraternities, problems of alcohol and drug abuse, and destruction of campus property is likely to make the student affairs committee a periodic focal point in coming years.

Another committee of increasing importance, according to some trustees, is the committee on long-range planning, often initially established in response to economic changes and demographic forecasts. The function of this committee is not to oversee ongoing activity but to analyze future possibilities and develop guidelines for future action.

How deeply involved in the content of issues these various committees become varies widely among the colleges and among individual board members. At Salinger, one trustee had his own staff do the research necessary to produce a sixty-page report on admissions and demographics; at Melville, on the other hand, even the Investment Committee is rather inactive and relies on the business manager to work with investment counsel and monitor the investment portfolio. This kind of reliance on the college staff, although unusual for an investment committee, is typical of trustee committees overall. Illustrative of the usual pattern of trustee-staff relationships and of the flow of information is this description by a committee chairman at Longfellow of the informal discussion that takes place among trustee "experts" in the committee setting:

> There is a staff person who relates to each committee, and the president rotates among each committee—he will often come in on a particular issue, and I would suppose that he was at the Buildings and Grounds Committee for a good part of the last meeting [because what to do with the old library wing is important now].
>
> Anyway, the president leaves it to the staff to relate to the various committees, and they do most of the groundwork. About a week before the meeting, the materials arrive, and in the last three weeks before the meeting the dean and I will be in conversation twice.

The members are very diligent and willing to discuss—we have a former professor and a medical man, and they are quite knowledgeable—the [board] chairman tries to appoint people to committees who have expertise.

Our recommendations are brought to the board, and there is a staff member present when our committee makes its report [in case there are questions].

In contrast to board meetings, so often described as businesslike and not conducive to discussion and debate, committee meetings are described as informal and conversational. The atmosphere is usually very friendly. The relationship between the committee chairman and senior staff member may establish a collegial atmosphere, and trustees welcome as well the opportunity committee meetings offer to become acquainted with the faculty and student representatives who may be present. When I asked how the student and faculty representatives figure in committee conversations and whether they could vote, the question was considered naïve, even irrelevant, the implication being that committees are places where decisions are made through discussion and consensus, or even the agreement to disagree, but not by vote; in any case, as one president pointed out, the students and faculty are outnumbered.[2]

Committees have the formal authority to make recommendations to the full board and also have a great deal of informal influence. As a consequence, whatever a committee recommends is normally—although not invariably—accepted by the board. There is an informal understanding among board members that as individuals they simply do not have time to learn about everything, and the committee system is a way of increasing their efficiency and effectiveness as a group. A Longfellow trustee explains:

What you have to understand is the complexity of things [that the board must consider]. Board members are segregated into committees where their talents can best be utilized. There is a general awareness of direction in other areas. Members should not try to do everything.

Variations in Committee Structure

Variations in the customary committee structure exist at several colleges. At Twain, the board has fewer than twenty members and often meets as a committee of the whole because trustees are unwilling to give up involvement in a broad spectrum of issues. Another variation is the creation of a trustee committee to meet directly with faculty or students. At Melville College there are two such committees, described by the board chairman as the board's "window to the campus." One committee meets with student government representatives; the other talks with an elected group of faculty, the "top faculty," the board chairman says. Interestingly, the president is not included at either meeting, a circumstance he describes with considerable tact:

> These committees are the way the board has of keeping in touch. They know [what's going on] from these meetings, which keep the board informed. . . .
> Occasionally it's a concern. It doesn't do for the trustees on that committee to hear things I don't know about first, but the faculty does let me know what they're going to be discussing.

Another variation among colleges is the length of tenure of committee chairmen. Most often there is a turnover in committee chairmanships every several years as trustee terms expire or as members ask to be relieved of the responsibility. Such changes are less frequent, however, at Cather and Salinger and also at Poe, where the board is said to function "like the U.S. Senate" with respect to chairmanships. At Poe the president and the board chairman want a committee head to be "activist and one who has time," so they can rely upon his or her availability to attend meetings and otherwise participate in board affairs. This philosophy results in long tenures by strong personalities, an outcome not considered desirable by all members of the Poe board:

> I want to be candid in making this clear. The board has become too acquiescent, too willing to leave everything to the five committee chairmen making the reports. . . . [A board becomes acquiescent] through the placement of dynamic people in chairmanships. It's almost like Congress; you don't buck the chairman.

Thus long tenures among the chairmen may reinforce tendencies to inactivity among members who are newer, younger, or otherwise less likely to take the initiative in board affairs.

The Executive Committee

As a powerful chairman may dominate a committee, so may the Executive Committee dominate the board. Among the boards in this study, four executive committees are relatively strong, and six are comparatively weak. It is interesting that the power of this committee seems to wax and wane over time, with its present status the result of the immediate past history of the institution. This pattern is illustrated in a story told by Longfellow's president: a previous president had "manipulated" the board by dominating the Executive Committee, which in turn ran roughshod over the board. Then, about eight or nine years ago, there was a "revolt" when the slate of officers brought forward by the Executive Committee was defeated, and a board chairman was elected from the floor. Shortly thereafter, the board's bylaws were rewritten, and the committee system was revamped to disperse power away from the Executive Committee to the standing committees. Now the only function of the Executive Committee is to review the president's annual plan.

The power of an overweening Executive Committee can be a very touchy and emotional issue. At Cummings, where ten years ago the Executive Committee was strong, there was also a rebellion, and one trustee recalls that during the meeting when the Executive Committee was abolished, "People got up and said they would resign if ever it comes up again." Even so, the Cummings Executive Committee has very recently been "resurrected" as a steering committee, although it is "going very carefully, with all kinds of reporting" to the full board. At Frost College, where the Executive Committee is very strong and the time required to be a full participant substantial, the president says it "tends to be a continuous group," although he does try to remove those who cannot maintain the required level of activity. Into their places he puts persons from the full board whose energy and interest, unless channeled through the Executive Committee, could conceivably find an outlet in the kind of revolt experienced elsewhere. Another factor mitigating discord at Frost may be the presentation of the Executive Committee as a permeable group; it meets in major cities up and down the east coast, and other members of the board are sent agendas and invited to attend.

Key Trustees and Their Influence

Trustees and presidents report almost invariably that under the auspices of the committee system, about one-third of the trustees are actually involved in the "work" of the board. These are the "active" trustees, those who can be depended upon to attend meetings, to read the background materials, and in other ways to give substance to the formalities of decision making. The committee system, however, does not represent the sum of power relationships within the board; rather, it works within an environment defined by the informal power and influence of individuals whom presidents often refer to as "key trustees." These individuals may or may not be numbered among the active minority and may or may not occupy a committee chairmanship, but they are perceived as important and influential by both the president of the college and their fellow trustees. The characteristics of key trustees vary relatively little from one board to another and thus lend themselves to stereotyping. Here they will be described in four categories—as the *nuts-and-bolts operator*, the *personage of power*, the *wealthy patron*, and the *elder statesman*—with the caveat, of course, that in a particular instance, a single individual may exhibit characteristics of more than one type.

Nuts-and-bolts operators are sometimes committee chairmen who, having been on the board for many years, are experts in the procedures of college administration in one or more areas, such as fund raising or student affairs. They are active trustees who work very closely with the senior administrative staff and do not hesitate to take the initiative in board affairs. A nuts-and-bolts operator is almost always an alumna or alumnus, is well connected among the alumni body, and was usually first appointed to the board as a candidate of the alumni association. Often these trustees live in or near the college town and in any case are frequently on campus, either attending committee meetings or participating in other events. They have multiple sources of information about campus life and are confident of having a fairly accurate reading of the campus mood. The chairman of the Student Affairs Committee at Cather is just such a person. In prior years he chaired the Finance Committee and recalls discovering that a former president had unintentionally misallocated funds. Now chairing the Student Affairs Committee, he is described by the chairman of the Cather board as having "got [a new dean of student affairs] and having made great progress there" and by another trustee as "a good local trustee who gives local guidance to the president." This key trustee has useful data for the board, such as a list of small college presidential salaries from which, he says, "We figure out what our guy is worth." He speaks of making an effort to talk to the president individually "to tell him when he's doing a real good job."

A second category of key trustee is composed of *personages of power*, whose achievements in the business or professional world carry sufficient public prestige to command automatically the deference of the board. To these individuals the board is prepared to give a respectful hearing, if the individual is interested enough in the college to speak up in board meetings and is persuasive when doing so. A personage may accept a committee chairmanship and be among the active minority or may attend meetings somewhat irregularly and be indifferently informed about the college. A personage of power on the Poe board is the dean of a leading graduate professional school and is described by a fellow trustee as a "hot shot whipper snapper . . . [who is] not strong because of money but because of his forceful personality"; it is said he grasps issues so quickly that it does not matter if he has read the background materials. Not all of the highly successful business and professional people on a board become personages of power, and the president of Poe remarks that there are chairmen of conglomerates on the board roster who are not influential in board affairs.

Wealthy patrons may be interested in the ongoing work of the board, as at Twain and Frost, where gifts of a million dollars have recently come from active trustees; or they may be inactive, perhaps because of age or conflicting demands on their time. This category is not limited to proven big givers but includes as well individuals who are thought to be able to give, although they might not yet have done so, such as the Thoreau trustee of whom it is said, "He could give millions." Also included in this category are individuals who may lack remarkable personal wealth but have access to corporate monies or have influence with foundation staffs or in other ways provide "contacts" that yield gifts for the college.

The *elder statesman* has typically achieved worldly success and is perceived by the board membership as having accumulated a lifetime of wisdom that not only illuminates issues but can materially assist the college. (These individuals are not to be confused with "life trustees," who may achieve that status through longevity and the awkwardness of asking them to resign.) On the Cather board, for example, there are two elder statesmen, one of whom is respected for his knowledge of the college and its traditions and the other for his lifetime of achievement and experience in higher education administration. At Twain, the role of elder statesman has been formalized by a change in the bylaws to provide for "emeritus trustees." Institutionalizing this very selective category is a strategy for continuing the participation of individuals who have reached the limit on terms of service, and a senior Twain trustee says, "It works; these are bright, experienced, talented men." A younger Twain trustee calls the emeritus group the "most powerful" on the board even though its members have no vote. As an illustration, he tells this story:

> [Emeritus trustee] is a real power in his own right. . . . I do all the work on honorary degrees—the research, the memos—and he'll be sitting on the outer ring of the circle and says, "I think this list lacks the proper luster; we need somebody to give the proper tone, and let's get [very

famous person]." And of course that person gets an honorary degree. If you can make a suggestion like that [and carry through on it], you don't need a vote.

Yet even among the select group of key board members, I was told repeatedly, a person's influence "depends upon the issue." A Cather trustee, himself a nuts-and-bolts operator, remarks:

> There are certain people whom everybody respects. [Personage of power], he's a partner in [investment brokerage] and he runs the investments and . . . nobody would cross him. And the same for [elder statesman]. And [another elder statesman], when he talks about traditions, people will respect his judgment—but (laughing) if he were twenty years younger, he'd feel the way we do!

A Twain trustee, also a nuts-and-bolts operator, makes a similar observation of his board:

> Leadership depends on the issue. While most of the board have views about the capital drive, I've been pro [a proponent of fund raising] for a long time, and people tend to listen to me. On personnel, [nuts-and-bolts operator] pretty much does it, and when he talks, you tend to pay attention.

As these comments suggest, trustees tend to think of themselves as a panel of consultants with diverse fields of expertise in professional areas such as investments, accountancy, and management, and in functional areas of the college, such as fund raising. Several trustees mused at some length on the strengths that particular individuals bring to the board, including this Poe trustee, who describes his own expertise as "group insurance and pensions" and offers the following observations of the Poe board membership:

> Jamison on the development program—a lot of work is done by Jamison. Neufeld is an accountant; he has an accounting background. Griswold has a good idea of what Poe is supposed to do [as an educational institution]. Ogden, he has a long background in finance. Middour made the arrangements with Conrail, and Davis has relationships with foundations.

Most often, the committee structure is the vehicle through which trustees channel their expertise, although several spoke of working directly with the president or senior staff and then leaving it to the president to present the results to a committee and take the issue through the requisite formalities.

Oligarchy in the Board Room

The existence of a relatively small number of active board members—about one-third—conforms to the so-called iron law of oligarchy postulated early in this century by sociologist Robert Michels.[3] Michels observed that within a voluntary organization—as with trustee boards— there is invariably an active minority in control. Furthermore, the structure of the organization, with its committees and division of labor, makes it possible for the minority to achieve the objectives of the group with the majority contributing little or nothing at all. Applying this insight to the small college board room, we may speculate that if a college president and board chairman make the committee chairmen and key trustees the focus of most of their attention, they will reinforce the influence of the minority and perhaps miss the opportunity to bring other trustees into the active and influential group. Of course, time is a powerful constraint upon the board chairman and the president, both typically very busy persons, and they know from past experience that if they can get the cooperation of a committee chairman, the committee members will generally follow along. The committee members, in turn, may (or may not) have a lively interest in the college but know they are not privy to information that the committee chairman may have. Feeling at a disadvantage in this respect and with time very limited at the committee meeting, they may simply go along with the committee chairman, just as the chairman of the board and the president—and Michels—predicted.

8 The Role of the Board Chairman

If leadership is defined as originating ideas, stimulating decision making in the direction one prefers, and articulating those ideas and decisions persuasively, then it is the president whom most trustees consider to be the chief figure in leading the board. "I cannot conceive of a board meeting without the president present," says the board chairman at Twain. "Meetings are nothing without the president," according to a trustee of Frost. Against this background, the role of the chairman of the board—the putative leader—varies somewhat among institutions. At Thoreau, the chairman is a wealthy and well-connected personage whose leadership is described as "symbolic" rather than substantive. Other chairmen are more enterprising and try in some way to mold the board, as does the Salinger chairman, who pays serious attention to committee memberships because he thinks that the matching of trustee interests with committee assignments determines how generous and active a trustee will be.

The Chairman as Mediator

Significantly, however, the common thread linking various conceptions of the board chairman's role seems to be the chairman's desire to reconcile conflicting views in a way that will protect the members' feelings but will also enable the formal and informal work of the board to go forward uninterrupted. The chairman of the Cummings board describes this mediating role as "play[ing] an active part to help see what might bring consensus . . . not control[ling] the board but guid[ing] it away from trivia which may be divisive." Similarly, the chairman of the Cather board remarks:

A chairman has to listen. You'd be surprised how many times I've listened my way to a solution. You know that course, "Human Problems in Administration"? What it shows is very simple, that most people just want to be listened to—that's 90 percent of solving a problem.

And it's important never to confront. . . . I think one of the principal things is to keep things from coming to a head. Wounds never heal.

Of course, the exact nature of a chairman's mediating role varies from board to board in accordance with personalities and interpersonal dynamics. For example, Longfellow's chairman, a corporate lawyer, suggests the objectivity of a judge when he speaks of presiding over "the interchange of ideas by the board and the president." Similarly, a Frost trustee remarks that when the Executive Committee and the president meet, "It's good to have the chairman there as a moderator." Certain chairmen, however, emphasize that their mediating role occurs in partnership with the president, as described by the chairman from Twain:

> On any given subject, the board might be split, and when that happens, it would be a matter for the committee of the whole. . . .
>   [The president] and I can sit there and can let people talk it out and air it out, and then the thing goes through, click, click, click. It's no good if you can't get people comfortable. I try not to ramrod.

Although board chairmen consistently imply that they wish to be receptive and even-handed in their responses to members' interests and opinions, they obviously consider themselves to be expert, more expert than other members of the board, on the issue of the president's leadership of the college. Therefore, the chairman functions not solely as a mediator in the relationship between the president and the board but also, when the occasion demands, as the president's advocate and chief defender against trustee criticism. At Melville, for instance, the chairman refutes criticism of the president by saying that "some trustees and others at Melville College have unrealistic expectations of what a president can accomplish." And at Faulkner, the chairman of the board has concluded that "the college presidency is the most difficult job in this country today," and he regrets that not all board members recognize this fact.

The Chairman as Educational Leader

Several board chairmen in the study feel a responsibility to provide leadership which transcends day-to-day bureaucratic management and personal diplomacy. These individuals have thought about the process of transmitting culture in an institutional context and about the place of their particular institution within American higher education. The chairman at Longfellow, for example, speaks of telephoning the president "just this morning" to say, "What the board has to face up to is the long view as to what the next ten years will require for the successful operation of the college . . . including academics, athletics, and buildings," a question he distinguishes from the five-year fiscal planning already accomplished. Similarly, the Frost chairman speaks of trustee interest in the question of "what Frost College is and what it wants to be."

Yet a chairman who tries to use these issues as a way of leading not merely the board but the entire college organization may not be successful; the collegiate tradition of participatory governance places many obstacles in the way of leadership from the top down. An illustrative story is told by the president of Twain:

> A new chairman of the board asked me to present goals for the college. I responded with an abstract statement that no one could argue with and concrete details of so much motherhood and apple pie that no one could argue with them either. And all of this was because I had developed a long-range planning committee on campus and I didn't want to short-circuit them.
>
> I had to be careful that I didn't get at cross-purposes with the campus planning committee, and I knew that [the board's] approving motherhood and God wouldn't do any harm.

Asked to give some examples, he replied, "Well, I said that we intend to remain small—no one can argue with that. And that we intend to remain coed—even among the alumni that's now noncontroversial." The implication is that overt leadership in the broad policy area of educational mission may be politically impossible for a board. On the private college campus, those who in theory are to be led may in fact lead the "leaders."

The Financi
Power of
the Board

> The ideal board would consist (
> twenty-five or thirty millionaires!
> —*President, Cather College*

No trustee of a private liberal arts college will fail to mention the board's role in the financial management of the college, and although the board will usually delegate to the president responsibility for developing the annual budget, a coterie of trustees is often intimately involved with the management of the endowment portfolio, the development of strategy and tactics for capital campaigns, and the design and location of the buildings for which capital funds will pay. In this respect the situation at Salinger College is not unusual: the chairman of the Finance and Investments Committee has professional expertise in finance—in this case as a C.P.A.—and the president reports that he and his internal staff have very little to do with the endowment. The president observes:

> More than student and faculty affairs, the trustees enjoy working with our large plant—establishing the property and its limits—and matters of finance. They know what to do and how to do it, and of these, the money is most important.

Although the majority of boards in this study have in common a substantial role in investing funds and overseeing current financial activities, individual trustees differ in their analysis of the college as a business entity, with some emphasizing its similarities to a profit-making corporation and others focusing on its differences. A trustee of Cummings remarks on the problems that colleges have but corporations do not:

> [Colleges have] no internal source of funds; they are victims of inflation and victims of lack of productivity; meantime, the cost of education will increase 2 percent greater than the CPI. Then there are problems of maintenance, deferred maintenance . . .

A trustee of Frost, in contrast, thinks that "the basic issues are about the same" between the collegiate and corporate sectors, with capital needs supplied in the one through gifts and in the other through bonds, and with timing and interest rates important in both sectors.

Making the Most of Assets, Human and Financial

More important than these differing views of the college as a financial entity are the dramatic differences among colleges in their assets, especially in the value of their endowments and the size of gifts that their pool of donors might reasonably be expected to make. These differences may be critical if severe inflation periodically recurs as the decline in numbers of high school graduates continues into the 1990s; in such a climate the prestigious colleges, with their large endowments and oversubscription of applicants, have a distinct advantage. From just such a position, the president of Twain can observe with guarded sanguinity, "It's not a matter of *whether* we'll survive, but how," thus acknowledging his feeling that the college will be affected in ways he cannot predict, but not direly so. Indeed, Twain would seem to be in an exceedingly strong position, with an endowment in excess of $80 million, with a board that contributed $3 million—an average of $200,000 each—to the recently launched capital campaign, and with good prospects among the alumni, as the board chairman notes:

> I have people in mind, people [who can be expected to make major gifts] and so do other board members. . . . We will need a seven-figure gift, but we have 400 alumni who could give a six-figure gift and that's where we'll get that seven-figures.

Similarly positioned is Cummings College, with a slightly larger endowment and a donor base sufficiently wealthy that a capital campaign has recently netted over $25 million.

At the opposite end of the financial spectrum is Cather College, with an endowment of $12 million. A capital campaign for $4 million to build a sports complex was recently launched, and one trustee explains that the proposed building program has been a subject of disagreement among board members, with one faction ready to go into debt to get construction under way and the other maintaining that funds should be raised before construction begins:

> The problem is going to be to get these people together and not have a dogfight. . . . Part of the board says we should not go into debt because our market is declining and over the next ten years will be down 25 percent or more in-state, where we get 90 percent of our students.

The problem is [that] these cash-on-hand folks are our most ardent contributors and we have to keep them happy, but students are communicating a need [for a recreation building] and we have to show these other trustees that our future admissions may be dependent on this new facility.

And this trustee goes on to name the seven colleges Cather considers its main competitors and observes, "They all have new facilities."

In fact, in spite of the economic crunch in higher education, the governing boards among the nonelite colleges in this study are approving major building and remodeling programs which they hope will enhance their competitive edge as the cohorts of high school graduates continue to contract. At Cather, for example, the capital campaign for the sports complex was eventually launched with the expectation that leadership gifts from the board would total no more than $350,000, a circumstance that prompted one trustee active in the campaign to telephone another alumnus who was heading the college's annual fund-raising drive:

I told him I need a gift of a million dollars, and he said, "I don't see it there." . . . But this time I pushed, and since I'm on a bank board, I went to talk to them this morning to find out about financing. The bank in Collegeburg will have to be the lead bank, but we'll need a [big city] bank as well. . . .

You have to ask yourself, am I doing the right thing? But a trustee has to be in a position of decision making, . . . [and] you learn you have to have faith in the day.

Typically, boards contemplating a major building program or other significant special expenditure are divided over the appropriate strategy for coping with fragile financial stability on the one hand and increased competition for students on the other. Even a board like Frost's, though the college is considered a very fine regional college on the fringes of "eliteness," grapples with this difficult question:

Our major decision is where the funds should go. Some feel that the endowment should be increased versus the physical attraction of the campus as the key to the continued life and strength and academic influence of the college. I'm on the latter side, though I like endowment too. There are two schools of thought.

Another Frost trustee remarks that the present endowment of about $25 million is "very sufficient for the number of students," although others "think the endowment is very low; there is discussion, but we get along."

The Trustee as Investment Counselor

It is not unusual for a member of the board either to serve gratis as the board's investment counselor or, through force of personality and expertise, to dominate the board's investment committee and to treat it, in effect, as a personal fiefdom. For example, a trustee at Poe reports that

> the chairman of our Finance Committee is brilliant and I admire him . . . but he does not like to be challenged. He wants to have his report accepted verbatim and gets irritable if he's questioned. Most of the board would not know that in committee he's challenged, and there are not many who will buck him in public.

At Cather, the partner of a New York brokerage manages the investment portfolio, and "he does it for free—nobody would cross him." At Longfellow, the Investment Committee is dominated by a single board member, and the college business officer puts in the calls to stockbrokers as directed, all of this without benefit of outside investment counsel. The chairman of the board, a corporate lawyer, is "not satisfied" with these arrangements:

> I think there may be real exposure here. I would continue to have an Investment Committee but would tie it in with investment managers. I wouldn't do what they are doing now any more than [my corporation's] board would do the investing for the pension funds.

At Cummings, where there had been "a dominant person—that's why we did so well," the Investment Committee formerly met every month to approve all sales and purchases, but now, having engaged outside managers, it meets quarterly and retroactively approves the transactions. "And maybe it's just as well," an experienced trustee concludes, "the advisors have all done well."

The Trustee as Major Donor

At Frost, the chairman reports that "trustees predominate in the management of the endowment, with no direction at all from the administration," although with the advice of outside investment counsel. Recently, the college was the beneficiary of the largest single contribution in its history, the gift of a present member of the board.

Once the gift was made, this donor trustee, according to another board member, "wanted to be involved in investment decisions, and some trustees didn't want him to dictate." The solution was to draw up a special agreement whereby this donor is given the authority to manage that part of the endowment comprised of his gift. And a trustee who participated in developing this arrangement observes:

> You have to take a practical point of view. You're not going to cross big donors if you can avoid it. And you're not going to upset the student body and the faculty, but you'll try to take [the donor's] concerns into consideration, not out of fear, but out of prudence.

Perhaps Frost's president is thinking of the implications of this "practical" point of view when he remarks that the Frost board "wouldn't accept an $18 million gift tied to a political belief."

In practice, however, moral principle is poor fodder for gift horses, particularly when it is not clear if, and to what extent, moral principle is being compromised. At one college in the study, a trustee offered to endow a chair in the social sciences on the condition that its first occupant be black. The president feared that the condition would violate regulations of the Equal Employment Opportunity Commission, but this worry proved groundless. Instead, a stumbling block materialized in the form of vehement opposition from members of the faculty who said that the board, in accepting such a gift, would be "getting too close to the operation of the college." Working with a faculty committee, the president argued that the proposed chair was filling a recognized need on the campus for senior black faculty members. When the faculty then contended that the condition attached to the gift was unfair, the president replied that their argument could be extrapolated to show that it is unfair to sociologists to recruit economists. The matter was resolved, according to the president, when the faculty committee was assured by the president that he would convey to the board the issues of principle which the faculty felt were raised by the gift.

The Trustee as Fund-Raiser

While the trustees interviewed for this study do not report a great deal of direct personal involvement in soliciting major gifts for their colleges, several report "hav[ing] the impression that others are out on the hustings." Of the four trustees interviewed who are chairmen of development committees, all mention numerous and lengthy telephone conversations spent in consultation and planning with the college's fund-raising staff, and it is clear that trustees feel a special responsibility for making a judgment about the "timing" of a capital campaign, that is, when it should be launched. Also mentioned is the board members' role in providing entrée and support for the college among corporate donors—with "more refusals than success," remarked the chairman of the Thoreau board. On the whole, however, trustees of private colleges seem to rely heavily on the president to be the chief fund-raiser, sometimes working in concert with the vice-president for development. Thus, securing a foundation grant to pay for an academic building now under construction at Salinger is credited to the president, "through," it is said, "the vice-president for development." At Cummings, the president is considered by trustees to be an effective fund-raiser, and he himself feels that the success of a recent capital campaign is owed in good measure to his efforts. The president of Poe acknowledges that he is the "strongest fund-raiser," but he later expressed second thoughts about this judgment, concluding that board members have better contacts at corporations, while he has better entrée at foundations.

Leadership in Giving

Although trustees look to the president to be the chief fund-raiser, most recognize the need for "leadership in giving" by their own membership if for no other reason, as the chairman at Longfellow observes, than "because foundations always ask, Is the board supporting this project?" However, some boards are less prepared than others to provide such leadership, either because the wealthy members are not motivated to give or because the board is relatively impoverished compared to the college's needs. A trustee of Cather says one-third of that college's trustees "have wealth or access to wealth," but he adds, "A lot are common, ordinary middle-class people" with a background in farming or an association with the church to which this now nonsectarian college has historically been related. At Melville, a trustee reports that the board is "weak in wealthy trustees" and while "some have been generous, others have not given what they should" and are "not educated" to make annual gifts. The Melville board chairman, according to this trustee, "feels he can't ask them to give because it's coming from above . . . [and he says] it's much better [to have the appeal come] from someone on the same level." Another trustee, this one from Longfellow, calls fund raising the board's biggest problem:

I don't think they really understand what the next decade is going to be
like: the ones who weather it are going to be those that recognize what's
coming and take the initiative.

    I wonder about the viability of the institution in the future, the
performance of the endowments; I'd like to look at the average return.
I'm concerned about fund raising and the fact that it takes five to ten
years to develop an effective program.

He goes on to remark that the president is cognizant of these problems
and says that Longfellow is fortunate to have a president so willing
to go out and try to raise funds.

    In spite of the opinion of some trustees that their own boards are
relatively poor in comparison with others or that their fellow board
members are too insensitive to the uncertainties of the immediate
future, most would agree with the Frost trustee who is inspired by
the belief that

    the college couldn't exist without the financial power of the board.
Without its financial strength and influence, it would be impossible for
the small independent college to exist.

In much the same vein, the president of Cummings College expresses
the feelings of other presidents and of trustees as well in observing
that the biggest problem facing the board is "the stewardship and
augmentation of resources. It's a constant job. The challenge is to
sustain the college and yet not drive the alumni gasping."

10 Recruitment and Retirement in the Board Room

The governing boards of private colleges are largely, but not totally, self-perpetuating. At the ten colleges in this study, about 80 percent of the membership is nominated by the board members, with the remaining 20 percent nominated by the college's alumni association. The alumni association's nominations are forwarded to the board for approval, which is virtually automatic. Through the director of the alumni office, who is normally an employee of the college reporting to the president or other senior administrator, the president is sometimes consulted about the kinds of persons from the alumni body who might make appropriate nominees. In just such a conversation, for example, the president of Twain College communicated his wish that a professional educator be appointed to the board, and in due course an educator was in fact nominated by the alumni association.[1]

Building the Board

Most presidents also play an influential role in identifying and recruiting candidates whose names are forwarded to the board by its own nominating committee; in this process the challenge, as many presidents phrase it, is one of "building the board." In this effort, presidents may not consider trustees to be terribly helpful because board members tend to recruit people similar to themselves, so that the "tone" of the board, as some presidents tactfully describe it, never improves. The president of Cather College comments straightforwardly, "I use the present trustees and their contacts to get new candidates, but the danger is that board members can become a clone, because board members choose like board members."

Similarly, the president of Frost has observed over many years that members of the board "just will choose people on their own level or lesser." He says that "the Nominating Committee just doesn't work well," and he has found that superior candidates "don't get put on" unless the president himself works "real hard to find those who are powerful." In fact, at most colleges the role of the president in identifying potential trustees has become deeply entrenched, as at Melville, where the board chairman fears that a stronger trustee presence in recruitment might offend the president:

> We do believe that trustees should recruit their own, but we haven't made it terribly explicit in a formal sense. It's a tendency toward a more structured separation of powers: the board should look after its own continuity. The president once in a while, I suspect, wonders [about this] because it has been traditional for him to recruit new members.

For presidents, the awkwardness of the recruiting procedure seems to vary in good measure with the prestige of the institution. Thus the president of Twain is in the fortunate position of knowing that an invitation would be considered an honor by its recipient and of feeling that "there are so many alumni you'd really love to have" on the board. In contrast, the president of Longfellow speaks of "delicate conversations" with "persons of stature," many of them non-alumni, in which he tries to probe the person's personal and financial interest in the college. And the president of Melville observes of these "awkward" preliminary conversations:

> Sometimes we just aren't excited [about that person]. But more frequently, they don't like us. . . . We want someone with a real reason to be interested. . . . Our confidence has to be strong that they will become involved [or else we won't ask them to join].

Finding promising candidates is a painstaking process for the presidents of some nonprestigious institutions whose alumni bodies are neither wealthy nor well-connected among the elites of commerce and the professions. Faced with this situation, the president of Thoreau feels he must look outside the alumni, and he is expending considerable energy in order to "strengthen the board to get ready" for the next capital campaign. He has recruited, among others, a prominent socialite to whom he initially appealed by saying he needed the man's help in getting "exposure" for the college. This socially prominent individual, once on the board, began inviting the Thoreau president to his annual Christmas party and "has drawn people out of the crowd" to meet the president. A more recent addition to the Thoreau board is a local man who owns his own business. Still, presidents recruiting non-alumni exhibit a certain wariness; they seem to want to exercise special care that the non-alumni candidates (and the alumni as well, of course) are sufficiently interested to make the college the beneficiary, as the president of Longfellow says, of "their influence, advocacy, and gifts."

As a means of broadening the college's base of support and of testing the interest and caliber of potential board members, several colleges have established a board of visitors or board of advisors composed of alumni as well as non-alumni. This group meets two or three times each year to consider various issues about which the president and board solicit their advice. At Poe, the chairman of the visitors is a member of the governing board; at Frost, the whole arrangement is informal and not linked to the trustees. At Melville, the president is thinking of establishing visiting committees to the various departments, rather than to the college as a whole. Yet regardless of the specifics of the arrangement, the major value of these advisory groups resides in their function as a "farm system," from which, says one president in a moment of wry candor, "you harvest the crop after cultivating it."

Alumni as Trustees

Because many college presidents, especially at nonelite colleges, feel considerable pressure to improve the prestige and financial power of their boards, they may be very quick to rationalize the value of non-alumni trustees.[2] But above and beyond this pressure, they seem genuinely to feel that unbridled or unmitigated alumni influence results in a board which is "parochial." This judgment reflects their frequent observation that at a basic emotional level, an alumna's or alumnus's opinion of what is right for the college is strongly influenced by what existed when that trustee was an undergraduate.

When trustees who are themselves graduates are asked about the kinds of people who make the best board members, they always specify alumni but are careful to add that the presence of a "more objective" viewpoint is valuable. These trustees have found that "you get the most commitment" from graduates, as suggested by this alumnus who is a member of the Faulkner board: "The most interested people are those who have spent four years here. They have a special memory that they cherish and a special dedication." In the same vein, the chairman at Salinger says that "you don't want all of them to be alumni, but you do want most of them to be, on the theory that they will be a little more dedicated." And the chairman of Cather remarks similarly: "We're not on the lookout for non-alumni—just the opposite. Our best performing trustees and contributors, with few exceptions, are alumni." Perhaps the most deeply felt defense of alumni as trustees comes from a Twain graduate and trustee:

It's unrealistic to think of the Twain board being anything but heavily alumni. If there were more non-alumni, it would be more like a corporate board, where you get expert but disinterested advice. But alumni are never disinterested.

Another alumni trustee of Twain, who was personally close to two non-alumni serving on the Twain board, agrees that a trustee who is not a graduate is more disinterested and "doesn't have the same stake," but he values the more "dispassionate and rational" attitude of non-alumni:

In this sense [controversial woman college president] was a very interesting trustee, saying, "You guys are taking yourselves too seriously." Also [famous labor lawyer]—he had a perspective and broad world view, [saying]: "Is this really what Twain should stand for in a moral, ethical, educational sense?" These were the kinds of questions he asked.

Still, most alumni trustees prefer their boards to be "heavily alumni."

A Thoreau trustee, not a Thoreau alumnus but chancellor emeritus of an urban university and a person with varied board experience, refers to non-alumni trustees as "sidewalk trustees." He says there is one function that only trustees who are alumni can fulfill:

They maintain and perpetuate a cherished appraisal of Thoreau, which is something I can't do. They know the institution's heritage the way I know [urban university]. [Urban university] is part of my body and soul.

This trustee, an elder statesman on the Thoreau board and an admirer of the Thoreau president, is sympathetic to the president's program for recruiting non-alumni trustees but is dubious of its outcome. He has observed that the non-alumni thus recruited do not always give of their own resources, although they seem willing enough to make "contacts" that result in gifts. He has the feeling "you can't count on what you're going to get" from non-alumni trustees, especially "if their interest in your institution is partly a result of some disaffection from their own alma mater." Similarly, an alumni trustee at Cummings who feels that the board is "parochial" and would benefit from the addition of one or two more non-alumni, says that, in his experience on boards and as a college president, it is "awfully hard to bring in an outsider and then expect him to be a big donor and then expect him also to be a fund-raiser."

One non-alumni trustee from Salinger is aware of the presumption that, not being a graduate, she is somehow "less dedicated"; yet she maintains that she is "very dedicated to Salinger." Perhaps her circumstances are unique. Although a trustee of her own alma mater as well as of Salinger, she is from a family long prominent in Salinger affairs and lives in Salingerville. She is disappointed that non-alumni "do not quite enjoy the camaraderie of alumni."

Not quite enjoying the camaraderie of the board is a theme sounded by all the individuals interviewed who feel themselves to be minorities within their own particular board rooms. A Twain trustee, for example, reports that a non-alumna on the board referred to herself and the other three members who were not alumni, not male, not middle-aged or older, or not white, as "outside the chosen." Such feelings are echoed by younger trustees, women, and the one black interviewed. For example, a twenty-five-year-old trustee and one of thirty-five, both with several years of board service, doubt that they are yet considered "full members" by certain other trustees. Women report feeling isolated and sometimes good-naturedly patronized with a "let's be nice to her" attitude. One woman who had asked during board meeting for details of the budget was told in good spirit after the meeting, "Oh Erica, you know any woman presented with this budget wouldn't be able to figure it out. . . . Women don't understand; men know about running the college." A different set of prejudices is perceived by a black alumni trustee:

> I approach things from a different perspective but end at the same place [as the white, male, middle-aged alumni trustees], and some people on the board, because I'm black, think I'm too conservative. They put a black on the board and expect him to yell and scream. . . . I do not see myself as representing black students, faculty, and staff, though I am more sensitive to them than most board members.

Affirmative Recruiting

Several trustees and presidents mentioned how difficult it is to find "qualified" trustees who are young, or black, or female, and preferably alumni. A "qualified" trustee, they seem to suggest, is able to contribute at last one among "work, wealth, or wisdom," and it is interesting that the women, the young, and the one black interviewed often speak of the differences between their own qualifications and these traditional requirements. For example, the black describes himself as having the "least defined career" on the board; a young woman mentions her difficulty in taking time off from work to attend board committee meetings, in contrast to established lawyers who think nothing of meeting at a club for a two-hour lunch; and two young but evidently successful lawyers speak of the costs of trusteeship with its travel and telephone calls, and one remarks, "I didn't realize the massive personal expense."

With respect to women as members of governing boards, many of the men interviewed—presidents as well as trustees—observe that they are looking for "good" women candidates. If the college has become coed only in the past fifteen years, the young women graduates who are in professional lines of work may just be beginning to achieve recognition and status, and in the meantime, the board often finds it must recruit a non-alumna. Ideally this woman either has a successful career or is distinguished by her selfless volunteer work and married to a man who has a successful career, and she should also be interested in the college. Although the aggregate national percentage of women on private college boards is 13 percent,[3] the percentage of women on the boards in this study is typically lower, eight of the boards having just one, two, or three women members, the equivalent of 11 percent or less. As these statistics suggest, a tradition of coeducation does not necessarily imply a significant female presence at the board level, and low rates of female participation commonly obtain at colleges which have long been coeducational as well as at those which, until more recently, were colleges for men.

One consequence of male predominance in the board room may be the perpetuation of the assumption that the president of the college will be "brilliant, attractive, handsome, with a beautiful wife." In the face of such expectations, efforts are being made by the American Council on Education and the Association of American Colleges, both higher education interest groups headquartered in Washington, D.C., to increase the number of women in presidencies, and they report that small gains have been made. Even so, my personal observation in interviews with forty trustees tends to corroborate the conclusion of the president of a women's college who suggests that

> until the composition of governing boards changes, the chances of women surviving the search process are going to be limited, except at extraordinary institutions that are willing to take risks. Sixty-year-old gentlemen see men as safer bets.[4]

The Local Trustee

Just as women, minorities, and the young are recruited in part to make the board seem appropriately representative, so too may a citizen living near the college be chosen to represent the interests of the community surrounding the college. Sometimes these "local" trustees, particularly if they happen to be alumni, will be looked upon by other members as having an intimate knowledge of what is taking place not only in the town but on campus as well; one of Poe's local trustees says that five or six members "ask me what the president's doing and who's saying what." Some local trustees find the position somewhat ticklish since townspeople may suppose that local trustees "are more powerful than they are," able to say one word and get the bats out of the library belfrey or potholes in the parking lot filled. At the same time, both local and out-of-town trustees recognize that living near the college may affect one's views, as suggested by this trustee who lives several hundred miles away from campus:

> [I would think that] living in the township would have an effect on your view of the college and possibly on yourself as a board member. . . . Vandalism, violence, other disagreements, when you're up here, are different in their impact.

Life versus Term Trusteeship

Arranging for the retirement of board members, whether alumni or not, may be difficult if they have been elected to the category of lifetime membership authorized in some boards' bylaws, or if they are on a board where the renewal of terms is so automatic that a trustee literally may not be aware when one term ends and the next begins. Years go by, and the desire not to offend these members, particularly those who are wealthy, often discourages the president and trustees from broaching with an aging benefactor the subject of retirement. As a result, the active members can begin to feel overburdened by superannuated individuals. At Poe, for example, the chairman of the board would prefer to eliminate the category of life trustee, make it honorary, and ask that honorary members not attend meetings. He feels that upon reaching the age of seventy-two a trustee should resign, but as it is, "the large number of life trustees almost dominates the board." The president of Poe, however, maintains that he has become a "convert" to the principle of life trusteeship because it preserves sources of wealth for the college. Even so, this president hastens to add, "It happens to work here, but I would never suggest it for other colleges."

Concern about the negative effects of unlimited years of service is presently at a fairly high level, and trustees and presidents at colleges which do not have formal or effectively functioning time limits on membership frequently say the issue ought to be examined. The few boards which have already made changes in their bylaws typically require automatic retirement after ten to twelve years, usually at the end of two consecutive terms. Sometimes there is a provision stipulating that after a hiatus of one year, the member can be reappointed, but a number of trustees say that during the off year, "you can lose some of your best members" to their other volunteer interests. A few boards have recently established a specific retirement age, usually seventy-two, and have abolished the category of life trusteeship while being careful to exempt those to whom such status has previously been awarded. At Twain College, as mentioned elsewhere, there is a limit of twelve years on trustee service, and a very select category of "emeritus trustees" has been created to perpetuate a formal relationship between the college and its most valuable former board members. Of course, it is not yet known whether these new retirement provisions will affect the stream of gifts to a college, but trustees on boards with revised bylaws are optimistic that former members will not be so offended as to change their wills and patterns of giving.

III Operating Styles of Boards

11 Trustee Judgment and the President's Recommendations

Although the organizational structures of the trustee boards at the ten colleges in this study are similar, these formalities obscure significant differences in operating style which distinguish one board from another. By the term *operating style* I refer to the board's informal decision-making processes and to the character of its relationships with the president and with campus constituencies. In practice, the board's operating style coincides to some extent with its formal structure and decision-making processes as they are described in the board's bylaws. The bylaws imply that the chairman is at the apex of a pyramidal structure which includes the other officers of the board, the committee chairmen, and the president of the college as the board's agent on campus.

Differences in Operating Style

A board's operating style arises in response to the central issue of trusteeship which is, Is the board (or is it not) going to substitute its collective judgment for that of the president, who is its agent on campus? As we have seen in the discussion of the board's evaluation of the president, many of the complications associated with resolving this question follow from the way information flows from the campus to the board: how, if the president is the board's official source of information, can trustees be confident they are getting an unbiased view of campus affairs? An illuminating instance of how difficult it can be to resolve this question occurred in the for-profit sector in 1972 when Arthur Goldberg, former Secretary of Labor, Associate Justice of the Supreme Court, and Ambassador to the United Nations, resigned as an outside director from the board of Trans World Airlines.[1] His action was prompted by the view that "in situations where [outside directors] are confronted with complex sets of facts, figures, analyses, and computer print-outs that are provided by management[,] [t]here isn't any way that [outside directors] can realistically substitute their judgment for management judgment."[2]

More than a decade later, Harold S. Geneen, a member of eleven corporate boards and formerly chief executive of ITT, offered a similar series of reflections:

> What can an outside director do? He can ask a question about what troubles him. It will be answered logically, if not in great detail. He will be told that management's answer comes not from the chief executive alone but from those in the company right down to the division involved in the problem. They know more than the director does about anything concerning the company. If one stubborn director continues, he is likely to be embarrassed by what he doesn't know. If he persists, he is casting himself in the role of troublemaker, and no one likes a troublemaker. So what is the director to do, except sit back in his chair, taste his cold coffee, and desist.[3]

To remedy this state of affairs, Geneen would "take all internal management members off the board, including the chief executive,"[4] while Goldberg suggests that outside directors of large corporations "be equipped with a small staff of consultants who have access to pertinent information to enable the directors to make informed judgments about the recommendations of management."

Similarly in the collegiate sector, although liberal arts colleges are obviously smaller and less complex than companies in the Fortune 500, there is the problem of how the trustees are to know what is really going on within the organization. In response to this situation, the boards in this study have adopted one of three distinct patterns, or models, of behavior. These patterns are here termed *operating styles,* and each is an expression of group norms[5] governing the sources of information it is appropriate for board members to consult about the state of affairs on campus. Since the sample of institutions is small, these three operating styles may not exhaust all of the variations in governing board behavior, but the models do have the virtue of isolating certain systematic similarities and differences among private college boards. In Model I, the board is the *ratifier* or "rubber stamp" for a president who may be very forceful, even domineering, in his or her relations with the board. In Model II, the *corporate* board, the intention of the trustees and president is to run the board as if it were overseeing a business corporation. In Model III, the *participatory* board, members have a great deal of informal contact with faculty and students as well as with administrators. What is common to all three models is the attempt to insulate the board from the temptation to tamper with the educational programs, and in this dynamic the president typically acts as guardian of the curriculum.

Predictive Value

I have found no way of predicting which college will adopt a particular operating style. The corporate style exists at Poe, which is the oldest college in the study, having been founded in the eighteenth century, and at Melville, which was established 120 years later. Neither the prestige of a college nor the size of its endowment are determining factors; for example, participatory boards exist at both Cummings, among the more selective and prestigious colleges in the country, and Cather, a so-called invisible college. What does seem to affect how a college board operates is, quite straightforwardly, the management style of the president and his or her willingness to educate the board to the degree of involvement he or she prefers; equally important, however, are the preferences, expectations, and experiences of individual board members (especially the "key" members) and the history and tradition of the board as an organization.[6]

While neither quantitative nor qualitative measures of a college are useful as predictors of the board's operating style, it is true that once a board member, the president, or a consultant senses the operating pattern—and this should not take a large sample of behavior—it is then possible to predict the kinds of group behavior that will occur. Anticipating behavior can be an advantage in managing the board and can also be useful for the individual who wants to become a more influential and effective member. Furthermore, comparing the three operating styles may suggest possible strategies for intervening, should there be a desire to change the board's customary patterns of activity.

12 Model I: The Ratifying Board

Thoreau is the only college in this study with a board whose conduct retains significant vestiges of the ratifying form, in which the board tends automatically to approve the president's recommendations. This form appears to have been common among boards at least until the end of the nineteenth century and to have persisted for the next fifty years at colleges where the increasing professionalization of the faculty did not undermine the presidency.[1] The ratifying style seems also to have recurred temporarily at colleges where a "heroic" president curbed faculty authority, however briefly, as appears to have happened some years ago at Melville College.

The ratifying board sees its role as providing a president for the college and then putting itself, as well as the college, in his or her hands. Board members' reliance on the president's advice is virtually total, and their relationships with other administrators, as well as with faculty and students, are superficial or almost nonexistent. Both the notion of having adequate "background information" and the concept of "full disclosure" are virtually irrelevant to board decision making. What is relevant is the president's recommendation, an attitude that puts the president in a strong position in relation to campus constituencies. In this setting, the board functions chiefly as an institutional support for the president, as the president's "sounding board," and as a repository of wealth and "contacts."

In the follwing case study, one can see the evolution of the Thoreau board as it moves from domination by a rather autocratic president in the heroic mold to a less rigid relationship with a younger president who seems willing to respond to the desire of some of his contemporaries on the board to engage in more thorough oversight.

The Ratifying Board at Thoreau College

At Thoreau the governing board has been dominated by the philosophy of a past president of the institution who, after a presidential tenure of twenty-five years, assumed a permanent seat on the board—and moved into a smaller office in the college administration building. As president, this man was "an autocrat but with a sense of humor, and a good scholar, too," according to a trustee who observed him from his own position as president of a nearby university. A strong presidency was the style appropriate to that particular era, this fellow educator observes, and he goes on to describe how Thoreau's president emeritus still makes it a point to lunch frequently with a wealthy businessman who resigned from the Thoreau board in moral outrage against a liberalization in dormitory parietal rules. In one sense, those lunches can be chalked off as the ritual of two old men whose time has come and gone; in another sense they are the touching residue of a heroic presidency, the president emeritus still cultivating friendship and courting wealth for the benefit of the college.

Thoreau, which was once in the country, is now engulfed by suburbia. It has 1,000 students and a reputation as a better-than-average middle-rank institution. The board, which was once dominated by Protestant churchmen, is now in the control of laymen of advanced years who were originally recruited by the president emeritus and by his successor, president emeritus II, who retired in the mid 1970s after a six-year incumbency. President emeritus II also retains a seat on the board. Each of these presidents went outside the alumni ranks in an attempt to locate for the board men of wealth and generosity. For president emeritus I, a good hunting ground was the governing board of a nearby national service organization, and members whom he recruited through this association and other contacts are now in their eighties and come to meetings when their health permits. "Dear old Mr. Turner," sighs one younger trustee, thinking of that benefactor's doddering gait as he mounts the stairs of Turner Hall to the board room.

The current president of the college, intense, but literate and open in manner, is a protégé of president emeritus I and a Thoreau alumnus and former faculty member. He speaks of the "regeneration of the board" as a "high priority" and says that he has "not succeeded in developing the board as much as I would like." It is interesting that he, like president emeritus I, has joined the board of the nearby national service organization and is trying in other ways to develop a network of wealthy contacts. The president has also resuscitated the board's Nominating Committee and has taken it through the development of guidelines for selecting new trustees. Recently, for example, he had his eye out for, and succeeded in recruiting, "an area businessman, head of a closely held firm, with a good business track record." Still, on a board numbering forty, the average age is sixty-six—"disastrous," according to the president.

The president says that "a strong presidency is seen as key by the board," which by tradition perceives its role as furnishing a president for the college and then submitting the college to his care and themselves to his judgment, "right or wrong," in virtually all matters. To illustrate this arrangement, the story is told of a trustee who, fifteen years ago, asked president emeritus I to explain what appeared to be the summary dismissal of the librarian and assistant librarian. President emeritus I replied simply, "The president has the power to hire and fire," and that was the end of the discussion.

There appears to be little interchange between trustees and members of the faculty; indeed, it is said that until the current president took office, the faculty "was treated like students." Two faculty members and two students attend each of the three yearly meetings of the board "by invitation," but these guests lack formal status both with the board and with the groups they might be thought to represent. In the view of one trustee, the board is virtually "anonymous" on campus. She feels that the board should take the initiative in making itself known but adds that "some of the older members would feel strange doing that." As a trustee nominated by the alumni association, she has also observed that the officers of the alumni association "don't seem to be interested" in board affairs, and none of the five trustees chosen by the alumni association makes a report to them.

Background information pertaining to substantive board decisions is often reviewed only by those few members who belong to the Executive and Finance committees, which meet jointly prior to the board meeting and then make recommendations to the full board. Information is not mailed to board members but is in a notebook at each trustee's place for use only during the meeting. Although trustees who do not belong to either the Finance or Executive committees tend to assume that these key committee members "know what's going on in terms of budgeting and finance," there is no evidence that the two committees' examination of financial and other issues is more than cursory. As the chairman puts it, "We are not an active board."

One member of the board, elected some years ago by the alumni association, is a lawyer of sixty who has practiced law in a small city and has a keen eye for human foibles. He has observed, with a mixture of resentment and incredulity, what he considers secretive and preemptory board practices and has spent several years musing, "There are well-recognized businessmen on this board—don't they consider this demeaning?" And he has concluded that "perhaps they don't want to be encumbered."

The selection of the current president, Dr. Albert Albans, illustrates graphically not only the arbitrary practices that have characterized this board in the past but also the tensions that are beginning to surface as newer, younger members object to past practice. In the late 1960s, when Dr. Albans was on the faculty and also a part-time administrator, president emeritus I, then in office, spoke to him privately about the possibility of his being considered for the Thoreau presidency at some time in the future. Three years later, when the president retired, Albans's name was placed in nomination by the secretary of the board, but there was no search committee appointed to evaluate candidates. Since a number of board members considered Dr. Albans "not ready," and since another individual was available as a "fill-in," Albans was not selected. By the mid 1970s, when this interim president tendered his resignation, Albans knew that the board leadership, consisting of the board chairman and two other key trustees, "had me as its priority." However, other trustees, including two interviewed for this study, knew nothing of this "unwritten agenda," although they did recognize that Dr. Albans was a leading candidate.

In the meantime, a search committee including faculty and student representatives had been appointed, and at the trustees' May meeting some months later, the chairman of the board said that the search committee still had five candidates remaining to be interviewed. He also announced a special meeting of the board four weeks hence to appoint the new president. Two days later, the special board meeting was rescheduled for the following Saturday, with no explanation given for the accelerated plan. One trustee recalls that before he went to the meeting, he "expected one name and one name alone—Albans—to be presented," and if that happened, he would consider resigning in protest against a process in which the governing board had not been presented with a slate of candidates from which to make a choice. What he found was that Albans had "obviously" been informed that he would be elected and in fact had his "acceptance speech" all ready for the occasion.

Another trustee recalls being dubious about the entire search procedure and taken aback by its outcome:

> I did not have confidence in the search committee, and I have mixed feelings about that whole episode. Individuals are dedicated to their jobs on the board, but we have had enough of the old guard, and I was very much afraid of more of the same. . . . At first I about fell out of my

chair when Al's name was presented. I was delighted—but good grief! And Al said later, "Didn't you know?"

But I didn't know, I didn't know if the board would be presented with a fiat or with two or three candidates to be informally interviewed.

She was "so surprised" she did not realize until later that several members had withheld their votes as a protest against the manner in which the nomination and election were handled.

In spite of this somewhat inauspicious beginning, Dr. Albans is well thought of for, among other things, bringing "fresh air" into the board room, and he is perceived by some of the younger trustees as being sympathetic to their frustrations with the "old guard." At a recent meeting, however, there was an "explosion." A trustee who had twice requested in vain that the annual budget be mailed out in advance once again saw it for the first time when she walked into the board room and opened her notebook. She was exasperated and angry, and when the motion was made to approve the budget, she asked "to go on record as abstaining" because she wanted time to study the document. She said to the assembled trustees that if the chairman of the board and the president of the college were afraid to give confidential budget information to board members, she could only assume they had more confidence in the secretaries who typed the budget than they did in members of the governing board. She recalls "gasps of horror" from some older members, but some of the younger men "with a different perspective, more demanding" spoke up in her favor. The chairman and former chairman of the board were present, and both suggested that they saw no reason why the budget could not henceforth be distributed in advance. Meanwhile, the president of the college said nothing, and in the silence, president emeritus I raised his voice in strong opposition. The impasse was bridged only when Dr. Albans was asked by the chairman to "find a means to work this out."

Although President Albans welcomed this new development, he admits feeling caught in the "cross fire" between the old and new guard on his changing board. His resolution of the secrecy issue has been quietly to send out in advance background information on the budget and other agenda items to those ten or so board members who might appreciate receiving it. At the same time, at future board meetings he plans to have a notebook at each member's place as usual.

As important as the "explosion" might be in signaling a trend toward fuller disclosure and more thorough oversight, it does not pose an immediate threat to the coterie of individuals who are recognized as most influential on the Thoreau board. These include both the college's legal counsel, who is identified by President Albans as "the heart of the board" and is one of the old guard recruited years ago by president emeritus I, and the board's vice-chairman, who, like the legal counsel, was once a student of president emeritus I and was recruited by him many years ago. The third position in the coterie seems to revolve among several trustees, depending upon the issue. This slot is filled variously by a trustee who is the retired president of a nearby university, or by a longtime trustee with a particular interest in finance and the physical plant, or by president emeritus I whose cues, according to Dr. Albans, "are of major importance in the functioning of the board." An example of the workings of the coterie was provided by the retired university president when he mentioned attending an operetta recently with president emeritus I and the college's legal counsel, and he said they were talking about college affairs and in effect "conducting official business."

The board chairman, a wealthy businessman described as a "symbolic leader" who "could give millions" to the upcoming capital campaign, is not a part of this inner circle. A graduate of an Ivy League university where since retirement he has become a trustee emeritus, he is also on the boards of two other educational institutions, and it is difficult to know where Thoreau ranks among his priorities. Concerned that his not being a Thoreau graduate might cause ill feeling among the alumni on the board, he agreed to be chairman for two years only and remarks of his stewardship, "I don't run the school." A man of goodwill—"The future is in our youth; I think they deserve the best"—he is an old friend of three of the important members of the old guard, and he is probably not going to support any changes in board procedure that would make them unduly uncomfortable.

Commentary

Perhaps it is a coincidence that Thoreau, with its rather old-fashioned, nonintrusive governing board, has a president whose public utterances suggest that the demands of the presidency have not overwhelmed his own intellectual life and personal philosophy of education. For example, in his report at a board meeting, President Albans observed:

> Like Cardinal Newman, I believe that, while our primary business is the sheer cultivation of intellect, the practical end of a liberally educated

mind is better service to fellow humans. Such a mind, as Newman saw, "brings with it a power and a grace to every work and occupation which it undertakes, and enables us to be more useful, and to a greater number."

In this manner the president provides expressive leadership while simultaneously working methodically to develop the network of contacts it will take to "build" the board. In the meantime, until these changes come to fruition, the board remains dominated by the "old guard," who see themselves as patrons of the president and emblems of the institution.

In today's activist climate with its emphasis on accountability, a ratifying style may appear to some to be outmoded and insufficiently rigorous, but such a judgment is not implied or intended here. As David Riesman points out:

All concerned, especially the president, are aware that the board is there, passing judgment even if ratifying, and can always reverse field and deny ratification, or ease the president out or not support the president. In other words, the anticipated reaction of particular board members may be crucial even on a board that seems to the outside to be a ratifying board and so views itself.[2]

13 Model II: The Corporate Board

In Model II it is the intention of the trustees and the president to run the board as if the college were a business corporation, and the majority of private college boards probably think of themselves as falling into this category. In this model, the board plays a role in framing those financial and managerial issues that also arise in the corporate world, such as capital expenditures, property acquisition, and management of assets. At the same time, the board expects the president to assume full operating authority, and the president, to a degree that varies from institution to institution, orchestrates and controls the board's contacts with others on the campus.

Six colleges in this study have governing boards which can be described as corporate. This model, in what might be called its purest form, is exemplified by the board of Frost College, the subject of a case study included here. At the other five colleges, the corporate style of the board is less distinct, and the real interest of their *modus operandi* arises from their attempts to live up to the corporate model they profess to embody. This latter group includes two colleges of the highest academic standing, Twain and Faulkner, and three colleges from the middle range academically, Melville, Poe, and Longfellow; they are discussed in the commentary following the case study.

The Corporate Board at Frost College

Frost College was founded in the late eighteenth century and is located in a small city. With an enrollment just under 2,000, it is academically selective; less than half of the students who apply are accepted. Although the college has a fine liberal arts curriculum, its special academic luster is based upon the quality of its preprofessional programs, especially in the areas of accountancy, medicine, and law. In the most recent graduating class, for example, every law school applicant but one was admitted to the law school of his or her first choice.

At Frost, the corporate operating style of the governing board is an outgrowth not only of the board's history and the personal inclination of present board members but also of the president's desire to exert a strong and guiding influence on trustee decision making. The president of the college, Dr. Robert (Bob) Roberts, has been in office for over fifteen years and speaks with ironic humor of the gray hair that symbolizes both his advancing age—he is sixty— and his long presidential tenure. Articulate and professional in manner, Dr. Roberts delights in telling the story of a former Frost board chairman who was also chairman of a Fortune 500 company. This trustee, very successful with his New York corporation, duplicated at Frost the governing arrangement he had established in his business. As a consequence, Frost has an Executive Committee of nine that meets six or more times each year, while the full board of thirty-five meets twice a year to ratify actions of the Executive Committee. There are attempts to keep all trustees informed of Executive Committee activities, and notices are distributed about the time and location of Executive Committee meetings in the event other trustees should wish to attend; however, it appears they rarely do. As one Executive Committee member explains, "The duty of the board as a whole is to ratify or not to ratify, but the Executive Committee digs into the background and helps to construct the issues."

In this arrangement, the president is the key figure. He controls the agendas of the Executive Committee meetings and is responsible for the development and distribution of background materials. He says that the Executive Committee engages in "plenty of inspection and disclosure" and that, from his point of view, the management of their activities is a "game of anticipation." His cardinal rule is "never surprise the trustees," and with each agenda item he tries first to warn them that it is coming, then to bring it to them formally, and third to remind them of its existence so long as it remains outstanding. He is on the telephone frequently with the board chairman and other key members to solicit their opinions and to keep them up to date. He recalls that once years ago he forgot to mention an item to the then-chairman, who promptly turned to him during the course of the board meeting and said in withering tones, "Well, I never heard about *that*!"

President Roberts speaks of having "hard discussions" with the Executive Committee from time to time. He says that trustees' thinking about the college is greatly influenced by "their own perceptions about their own business," and his board, he feels, is interested mainly in such things as "quick ratios, assets, fund balances, and deferred maintenance." Because of their outlook, he sees himself as a "translator" who has a "special obligation" to help trustees understand student behavior and faculty curricular matters, and these he tries to translate into indexes the trustees will respond to:

> It's not very often you can get trustees' respect for the faculty's professional activities, because they are interested in green grass and buildings and tangible things. . . . [So] I tell them about student placement records and alumni attainments.

In these and other areas, Roberts sees himself as "forcing upon [board members] the education they need," and the results of his tutelage are clearly evident in the observation of a trustee who says, "Our education departments do a fine job, and a very high number go on to graduate school—medical, law, that sort of thing." Perhaps the president's translations have been more successful than he thinks, or perhaps his perception of trustees as not interested in, or understanding of, educational affairs is mistaken, for three of the four Frost trustees interviewed expressed a particular interest in faculty and students and the college's educational goals. The chairman of the board, a senior operating officer in a Fortune 500 company, ranks educational issues with financial issues as a major board responsibility, and he professes more concern about "see[ing] that the college is being kept as liberal arts and humanities" than about "keep[ing] it on a financially sound basis." He says that

> there is consensus [in the Executive Committee] about the kind of school Frost College should be, but our most heated discussions are on one topic, which is one department not getting out of balance with another, which is easy to do.

Ultimately, however, the rationale for trustee concern about educational matters is financial, as the chairman explains: "The message from trustees [to the campus] is loud and clear: discuss the make-up of the student body and the disciplines we are studying. These decisions have an economic impact." Indeed, the board's financial responsibility is an underlying theme in much of the conversation of Frost trustees. They see the board not only as the fiduciary of present assets but also as a source of additional wealth, and they candidly admit that in selecting new trustees, "you can't ignore the wealth." This consideration seems to embarrass some members but not the board chairman, who speaks enthusiastically of a friend whom he hopes to recruit for the board, a man who "has enough [money] to enjoy himself this way."

Since the Frost board considers its activities similar to those of the board at a for-profit corporation, it relies heavily on the president for guidance in making decisions, but even so, the chairman likes to conceive of the Executive Committee as "where the thinking is done. . . . [We] pretty much shape the policies." As an example, he mentions that the Executive Committee has initiated recent discussions of the college's mission—"what Frost College is, and what it wants to be,"—and other trustees offer their own examples of what they consider to be policy-level contributions by the Executive Committee, including:

> . . . the new method of handling the endowment. We [trustees] did the whole thing—the portfolio mix, the selection of investment managers, the method of measuring managers.
>
> The budget has greater review and is not always accepted in the way the administration first presented it.
>
> The Buildings and Grounds Committee did a physical inspection and put together methods of energy control. It saved 41 percent.

Yet almost in the same breath with assertions that they "shape policy," Frost trustees say that the president and other senior administrators are very influential in molding trustee opinion. This is how the chairman describes the interplay of administrative influence and trustee decision making:

> We try to develop a consensus among trustees as distinguished from the administration. . . . The administration does direct the board's thinking, except for two or three of us. . . . They lead us, but we're not rubber stamps. We don't always agree with what they say.

Another trustee remarks that "there are very few times that I can catch the administration unprepared." This trustee finds that the administration "does its homework," and he is usually impressed with, and persuaded by, the quality of the analysis:

> [I try to be] critical and sensitive. I look for areas that I can bring expertise to a college problem. . . . I will say, are you sure you want to do this, and Bob [the president] has already had a look at that area and has a reason it won't be a problem.

Another trustee, from his vantage point as head of the Buildings and Grounds Committee, admits that most of his committee's recommendations originate in the administration because "there is so much with which you have to become familiar" before you can make sensible decisions about things like the removal of trees and buildings. He describes his committee's function as one of "discussion and understanding and review."

In contrast to the trustees' pride in their tangible contributions to policy and program, the president has a process-oriented conception of the board's role:

> An institution such as this can weather changes of president, but its real continuity and strength lies in the board. The board has a personality that extends over a long period of time.

One influence on the personality of the board, Dr. Roberts explains, is the caliber of individuals recruited:

> I try to find men who like to live together and live at high levels—that's what motivates them to come to meetings. At the start, this board was a bunch of dead ducks, and they will choose people of their own level or lesser. Now when [the senior vice president of a major chemical company] comes, other people come because they want to be at a meeting where he is in attendance. Same with [the founder of an oil company]. You work hard to find those who are powerful; I have sought, ingratiated, solicited, pleaded . . . and it goes unnoticed.

If the president's efforts to build the board have gone unacknowledged, they nonetheless appear to have had an effect on how Frost board members view themselves. One trustee, an entrepreneur who at age fifty has the means to be retired, confesses:

> I guess I've been bit in awe [of the board], like a young boy going on his first date. It's fun to watch the dynamics of the College in terms of its history. It's fun to rub elbows with that crowd. Perhaps I don't feel that I fit.

Another board member, initially appointed as a nominee of the alumni association, was so conscientious during his first term that he believes the chairman and president "felt obligated" to ask him to stay on as a "term trustee." He finds Executive Committee members and their conversation stimulating:

> The Frost board is made up of men and women who have had in their own life-style responsibility for management of something. . . . The Executive Committee has businesslike meetings and exciting discussions.

Another adds:

> The tone of the Executive Committee meetings is all business—I'm the only one that rocks them up! . . . There are some pretty aggressive hard noses on the Executive Committee, and they don't give in too easily. We

meet for two or three hours at a stretch, over lunch, and until 4 or 5 o'clock. It's an active, participating group. I'm the weak link because I can only attend 75 percent of the time.

The board chairman, equally enthusiastic, speaks not of status and excitement but of the pleasures of fellowship:

I try to make the meetings interesting and to provide some satisfaction in getting together. Sometimes three or four or five of us will stay over-night and talk things out. . . . We get down and kick things around. . . . I walk away from most meetings feeling satisfied. The college is run well, and I consider many trustees as friends.

Overall, the Frost trustees appear to feel that they are engaged in a well-organized, high-level activity. It is not the sort of mindset conducive to nit-picking and to second guessing the president, as this board member explains:

If you get involved with the troops, your objectivity is lost. That [kind of involvement] is Bob's worry. You could screw up the administration. You don't know whether you are at the opposite pole from the administra-tion. Most anyone who [complains] is chafing under a policy decision; there's always someone for whom a business policy pinches, and you have to accept that. I have to run a business that way; why shouldn't a college run that way?

While no trustee interviewed at Frost seems tempted to "get involved with the troops"—with faculty, staff, or students—two trustees speak warmly of the opportunity on committees to develop contacts with a couple of students, and two other board members speak somewhat wistfully about "not [having] much direct contact with the faculty." The president in turn sees a danger of possible confrontation between the board, which has the formal authority to start or eliminate programs, and the faculty, which actually provides the instruction. He believes that if a board is going to make a decision about faculty or curriculum, it must "have the power to make [the decision] stick." To illustrate, he tells the story of his mentor, once the president of a state university. That president, using the powers of his office and of the governing board, changed the curriculum, but shortly after he left the campus for another presidency, all the changes were undone. And Dr. Roberts concludes, "An institution like Frost College can't stand much of that." He says that the faculty is now considering a curricular revision, that its most recent vote was a very close 54 to 48, and that "the board will not intrude in this process." He sets great store by procedures in the faculty handbook which lead to an "inevitable process" in areas such as tenure and curriculum. These areas he distinguishes from issues such as faculty salary increases, for which development of the decision, not merely its ratification, is a legitimate function of the board.

Although trustees of Frost rely on the expertise of the president and respect his office and the power he wields, in board matters they are careful to honor the formal authority of the chairman, as this trustee's remark illustrates:

> I don't know how often I call the college or committee members—maybe two, three, four times a week. But if I want something done, I call the chairman. Nobody tries to upstage anyone else. There's no backstabbing.

The chairman himself comments that the board has "some prima donnas with half-cocked ideas," but he stands back and tries "to let others argue the issues out." This approach, he feels, has a positive outcome for the college:

> The secret of an active board is to make them feel they have a voice. . . . One doesn't want to expose stupidity in a meeting. . . . It takes a man awhile to understand meaningfully about the function of a college and the role of trustee. Then they contribute more.

In addition to his interest in seeing that board members feel "satisfied" after meetings, the chairman says that "one of the principal roles of the chairman is to minimize the shock of [presidential] transition." Thus, although he "dread[s] Bob's ever leaving the school," he feels duty-bound to make preparations in the event of the president's retirement or early departure because of ill health. What he has in mind is a specific plan inspired by a management development program in his corporation. The object of the program is to identify the best-performing and most promotable executives, and the purpose of establishing a similar program at the college would be to identify the successor to the president: "The point is to avoid that outside candidate." The president is aware of this concern about succession, which he says is revealed by two recurring trustee questions: How's your health? and Why don't you appoint a provost? But the trustees, he says, are mistaken in their belief that an heir apparent should be appointed as provost: "That won't go down [on campus]. He wouldn't even be a leading candidate. What they don't understand is that I can't choose my successor!"

Ironically, the succession that the president himself is concerned about is the board chairmanship. Dr. Roberts is certain the present chairman does not recall that he is expected to retire from board leadership when he retires from his corporate position this year. This condition is stated in a letter the president once wrote to the board chairman, but there has been no communication on the subject since. Otherwise, the president seems unperturbed about the process of moving trustees in and out of positions of authority. New trustees are apparently given an opportunity to work on committees, and those with interest in the work and the time to attend meetings are likely to be asked to join the Executive Committee. But the president observes that "as the work gets hard, the honor [of being a trustee] recedes," and from time to time he will get a phone call from someone who cannot keep up. To this person he says it is easy to say outright, "Please, I need that chair." With a trustee who has poor attendance but does not offer to resign, the president might look for opportunities in meetings to say meaningfully, "I'm sorry you weren't here when we discussed this at length." A trustee who has watched the president in these situations describes him as "a master at handling them"; a person becomes "glad to step down."

One personnel matter of particular delicacy at Frost involves the board's procedures for compensating and evaluating the president. The president describes his situation by saying, "I serve at the pleasure of the board, but I have a contract covering my compensation." He goes on to explain that at his suggestion, an Executive Committee on Personnel has been established and includes the board chairman and four members of the Executive Committee. They meet with the president once a year and give him a "good grilling," presumably about the activities of the senior staff and his own activities. Even so, Dr. Roberts makes it clear that he "[doesn't] believe in a formal final evaluation: the Kingman Brewster seven-year evaluation is a phony; it can't come out negative. . . . I'm evaluated every day of my life." Dr. Roberts believes that the publicity associated with Brewster's performance review effectively eliminated the possibility of a negative evaluation.[1]

A Frost trustee remarks that evaluation "is a difficult area for the president." Although this trustee has no direct involvement in setting salary and assessing performance, he recalls that the procedures relating to presidential evaluation were reviewed "very thoroughly" three years ago. Another trustee elaborates:

> Eight months ago a committee reported to the Executive Committee about evaluation and compensation. It concluded that the president was doing a good job and recommended a remuneration scheme. One reason this was done was because Bob wanted a deferred compensation arrangement.

The board chairman says that adjustments in compensation are made every eighteen months and that he himself is responsible for sitting down with the president one-on-one to discuss compensation and performance.

Overall, Frost trustees appear very pleased with the college's prospects for the future. One trustee says flatly, "We have no problems"—an optimism somewhat more trenchant than that of his colleagues, who at the very least express mild concern about the challenge of "keeping the college on a financially sound basis." Another concern seems to be the financial impact of federal and state support, especially through student aid. One trustee speaks of not wanting to get "mired down in too much government aid. I ask the college for figures on this. I don't want [eventually] to have to go hat in hand to the legislature." And another trustee adds with some fervor: "We at Frost College believe in the small independent college. . . . Trustees feel a challenge in serving an institution that is free of government."

Commentary on Other Corporate Boards

As the relationship between trustees and the president at Frost College suggests, a leading feature of the corporate operating style is its members' perception that, as the chairman at Longfellow observes, "The board should relate to the president and not run the college. . . . The CEO has the responsibility to operate; his is the management function." This chairman is influenced not only by his professional experience as legal counsel to the board of a billion dollar corporation but also by his observations of a previous presidency at Longfellow, during which the office of student affairs was "surrendered" to its board committee. Although another Longfellow trustee admits that "we have problems with members who impinge on the president and his staff," and although the president says he must "work to keep [the trustees] from administering," the board has recently agreed to reduce the number of its meetings from five to four each year; this suggests that a standard of lesser trustee involvement is being successfully established.

At Twain, one trustee describes the relationship between the president and the board as "complementary," a term reminiscent of the participatory mode from which this board seems to have evolved recently:

The board's relation to the president is not heavy-handed, but complementary. The trustees do not and should not be involved in day-to-day

affairs unless they accumulate in a reversal of circumstances. We delegate to the president in all matters: choice of curriculum, hiring of
faculty . . .

A "reversal of circumstances" that occasioned the board's direct
involvement in administrative matters occurred several years ago
under a previous president. At that time, the president was unable
to negotiate successfully with the faculty to revise their salary schedule,
and the board dispatched one of its members, an experienced
management consultant, to the campus to meet with the faculty and
resolve the issue—and he did. Since then, however, there have been
changes in the board's membership, a new president has taken office,
and a new attitude is said to prevail among the majority of board
members:

> We want to be told about problems, but ideally the president says "I'm
> handling it this way.". . . The board doesn't want problems, it wants a
> well-oiled machine. We want to know that the president is on top of
> things [and] that he works out problems with the least amount of input
> from the trustees.

Still, among some members of the Twain board, there is sentiment
favoring deeper and broader involvement, and the trustee who says
that "[our board] is an active board, but there is a clear and enforced
understanding that we keep out of administration" also says that
"everything has gotten so bloody complicated that quarterly meetings
are an anachronism":

> In 1930, you didn't have a whole lot to do four times a year. But now
> with the federal and state government and the campus active and our
> own affirmative action program and ERISA [federal regulations govern-
> ing retirement benefits], it seems to me that four times is not enough.
>   What it means is that the plate is too damn full when we go, and we've
> had to lighten up the plate. So, more and more we have skated gingerly
> across the top when we could have been more constructive. I would have
> more meetings.

When members of a corporate board become very active, they tend
to display a sense of limits about how much and in what areas a
trustee may appropriately become involved. At Poe, for example, one
trustee feels that the board's relation to the president should be
developed within the framework of "monitor[ing] him and assist[ing]
him to carry out his plans." In the spirit of offering assistance, this
trustee has determined that the college should evaluate architects
more thoroughly, and since he is retired and has ample means and

leisure, he accompanies senior staff members in their travels to look at buildings. He distinguishes his participation in the selection of an architect, a traditional interest of trustees at many colleges, from "evaluating a professor," which the board "insists" be done by the Poe faculty and outside experts according to established policy. He is mindful that there "is a limit to what you can do" as a trustee and that your "usefulness can rapidly disappear." This same sense of restraint is also demonstrated by the Poe chairman, who says, "When people say to me you ought to do so-and-so, I say that's for the president to decide."

The corporate operating form seems to work best at a college where there is a president who takes a strong but not autocratic hand with his board—a president who keeps the board informed by plying it with background information but maintains sufficient influence to assure that all of his recommendations are adopted. An example of this kind of presidential clout in action has recently occurred at Poe. There, an active and influential trustee who is heading up a task force on the sensitive issue of fraternity life has felt it prudent to talk with the president in advance in order to make sure he will not "torpedo" the task force report this trustee will soon bring to the board. The president of Poe, for his part, cannot recall ever having had one of his recommendations turned down by the board, but even under these most congenial of circumstances, there remains some tension between the president's apparent preference for what one Poe trustee calls an "acquiescient" board and the desire of some of its members "to bring the board up to speed."

Many members of corporate boards are torn between the viewpoint of a Melville trustee that "having picked the president, the board should back him up—he's the CEO" and the desire to exercise conscientious oversight and not slide into the mold of a "rubber stamp." At Melville, the tenure ratio is an issue on which the corporate desire to back the president has so far triumphed over dissenting trustee opinions:

> We accept the recommendation of the president with respect to tenure, although we're not satisfied with the policy on the level of tenure. So we rubber-stamp, in keeping with our policy of backing up the president.

Although faculty affairs is an area where governing boards rarely play an influential role, the corporate board is especially discreet in not violating this tradition. This hands-off posture can be attributed not only to trustee restraint, but also to presidential diligence in deterring any lapses in trustee restraint, and to the faculty's well-established authority over curriculum and its power—if not the formal authority—to control tenure appointments. For example, the tradition of ratifying tenure recommendations coming from the faculty through the president has been very strong at Poe, and the trustees realized rather belatedly that the faculty was recommending tenure for 90 percent of the candidates, that the board was approving these proposals, and that the college was rapidly moving toward a 90 percent tenured status. Once this pattern was recognized, the board, in a conscious attempt not to appear to interfere in faculty affairs, asked the president and the faculty to develop a new tenure policy which would help the college avoid becoming "tenured up." Over a two-year period, under the influence of a strong chairman of the trustee Committee on Educational Policy, and with broad participation from faculty members, a tenure policy was formulated and then approved by the board. Recalling this process, Poe trustees are very pleased with how clearly they were able to communicate among themselves and with the faculty that it is the board's function to see that tenure ratios are established, but not its function to evaluate the qualifications of the individuals eligible for tenure.

Although presidents with corporate boards are sympathetic to the board's role in establishing tenure ratios, they discourage trustee involvement in other matters relating to the curriculum or faculty members. The president of Longfellow, himself a former academic, feels so strongly about this principle that he says, "Tenure is not considered by the board," by which he signifies that the faculty's recommendations are automatically ratified. At another college, where the faculty is now reviewing the curriculum, the president says he wants the trustees to be "knowledgeable but not meddling" in curricular affairs, and he emphasizes that the "faculty has the final word over educational matters."

In addition to guarding against any tendency by trustees to tamper with the curriculum or with specific tenure appointments, most presidents of colleges with corporate boards give trustees the impression that the only contacts board members properly have with faculty are formal, as at a committee meeting, and anything more would be "meddling." Thus many trustees see faculty members, and students as well, only in committee meetings and on special occasions, typically during a certain trustee meeting each year when the president hosts a dinner to which faculty and sometimes students are invited to join the board members.

An unusual situation involving direct official contact between faculty members and trustees exists at Melville College where, as described earlier, trustees meet with a faculty committee and also with a student committee without the president being present. As an example of the committees' activities, the president mentions that at a recent student-trustee meeting, the students put "a lot of heat" on an administrative decision to reduce the staff at the infirmary. Though this item was not on the board agenda, members of the board, some of whom had previously learned of the administration's action through the student newspaper, "wanted to know what's going on" and asked the president to explain the reasons for the decision.

All in all, the president with a corporate board is in an awkward position regarding the relationship of students and faculty to trustees. On the one hand, the president is the chief defender of the integrity of an educational process based on freedom of thought and expression; on the other hand, he or she may be wary lest the professors and students who speak most freely to board members are those most apt to criticize the president. And indeed, it seems inevitable that at least some negative feelings about a president will exist on any campus because, as the chairman of the Faulkner board observes, there are more constituencies than a president can possibly satisfy at once, so they "all become antagonists" at one time or another. It remains for the president to cope with this problem as best he or she can, and the technique used by most presidents with corporate boards is to discourage informal contacts between faculty or students and board members and to try, insofar as possible, to exert a substantial amount of control over whatever contacts do take place.

While some members of corporate trustee boards tend to "think of the college as a multimillion dollar business, and if the ship is not run as tightly as if the place were Kodak, then they say give the president the sack," many of the trustees I interviewed from corporate boards do not share fully in this attitude. Although they continue to use "corporate" rhetoric and although they may wish that effective lines of control extended from the board room through the president's office and on down the line, they know that colleges simply do not run that way. Indeed, the comments of the chairman of the Melville board, who is chief operating officer of a Fortune 500 company, suggest that trustees whose highest value is a "tight ship" misunderstand not only collegiate organizations but business organizations as well, because they "imagine that presidents in general play a larger role and are more omnipotent than they are":

A college president can't give to very many people a direct order; he obviously has to coax and wheedle. . . . But I'm not so sure a college is all that different from a business organization. A corporation is not an army. In most modern business organizations, one has to be a broker of diverse and conflicting views. That's much of what modern management is all about.

A more common conclusion by members of corporate trustee boards is that the designation "chief executive officer" is simply an incomplete description of how in reality the president relates to the rest of the organization, as a trustee on the Faulkner board observes: "The president is the CEO of the administrative line, he presides over the faculty, and he is the chief development officer. He wears many different hats."

This "different hats" perception of the presidential role is especially prevalent among the corporate board's active members, who have found that their CEO actually functions as something more—and less—than the title might imply. In this situation, so much more ambiguous than the organization chart indicates, seasoned trustees maintain that the best contribution any member can make to the board and to the college is to ask "pointed questions." And, adds one senior Twain trustee with a developmental bent, it is the responsibility of experienced board members to educate the newer members about "what the right questions are."

14 Model III: The Participatory Board

Boards operating in the participatory mode, including Salinger, Cummings, and Cather, are more likely than those in the ratifying and corporate modes to engage in activities the president may feel are interfering in the administration of the college. One president describes the attitude of these board members as proprietary, and it is true that most participatory board members are alumni who seem to have a highly personal stake in the success of the college. If it was an elite college when they attended, they are determined that it remain so; if its future is problematic, they are determined to beat the odds. The chairman of Salinger's board gives voice to this undercurrent of feeling when he observes that the relationship of a college to its students "is sort of like raising a kid. You take the student in, and when he gets out, he takes care of you in your old age." The participatory board is not so much taking care of business in corporate style as it is taking care of the college in familial style, as is illustrated in the case study below and in the general commentary that follows.

The Participatory Board at Salinger College

When Dr. Eugene Griswold assumed the presidency of Salinger College nearly a decade ago, the college had a debt of $12 million and an endowment of $6 million. To his astonishment, he found the board of trustees unperturbed by these financial problems. During his tenure, the debt has been reduced almost by half, the endowment increased by more than 100 percent, and the enrollment level maintained, although there is some evidence that the quality of incoming students' credentials has declined. The college is situated in a semirural setting with little public transportation available to the industrial city that is the nearest metropolitan area. One hundred years ago, according to the chairman of the board, the college "turned out a lot of ministers and lawyers," developed a fine academic reputation, and, he says, "that reputation lingers on."

President Griswold says the board is composed almost exclusively of alumni and is "jealous of its prerogatives," with an Executive Committee that meets monthly. He speaks to the board chairman two or three times each week by telephone, and he mentioned an "oil lease deal" that had required ten telephone conversations during the past month with a trustee in a distant city. In the early minutes of our interview, Dr. Griswold remarked that the board contributes "nothing" to the internal operations of the college, but as the visit drew to a close well over an hour later, he observed, "The Executive Committee runs the college, not the faculty or students." The board chairman, in turn, also says that "the alumni are very influential and in essence run the institution," and he describes both the Executive and Property committees as "up on day-to-day affairs." The Executive Committee is also described—by a trustee who is not a member—as "the power behind the board" and a "bunch of good ol' boys," all of them graduates of the college.

Another trustee, an alumnus who is not on the Executive Committee, says there are "two mentalities" that influence how any board goes about its activities: "We hire the president to care for the administration and if he does not perform, we get rid of him. Or, the board tries to do it, tries to make every decision." The Salinger board, he says, takes the middle course between these two alternatives, but he observes that it is definitely a "working board."

This trustee, executive director of a large social service agency, then goes on to describe his own role in the search now under way for a chairman of the college's department of psychology. The retiring chairman had taught in the psychology department and had also filled the position of college psychologist. The president, according to this trustee, wants to continue the present arrangement and to recruit one person to fill both positions, whereas the trustee wants to divide the position and hire two people. To this end, he has used his professional contacts to locate potential candidates and has "screened the names, and all the ones that look good [I have sent on] to the president and the search committee." He estimates that he has spent some eight hours a week, for a period of several weeks, on this endeavor. With an unusually busy schedule of late, he has had some difficulty in getting to board meetings, but when the minutes arrive in the mail, he reviews them and telephones the president with any comments or questions that occur to him. This trustee has been on the board for twenty-three years and for some of that time lived in Salingerville, where he had "indirect communication" about the college through a number of faculty members he knew socially. Now his contact is "less frequent," but he says there are "enough [others] living in town that we can get enough free and open discussion."

Nine trustees, or one-quarter of the board, make their homes in Salingerville, and the president says he has made them understand that all of their contacts with the campus are to be made through him, a distinction he does not seem to insist upon for out-of-town trustees who might, for example, telephone a member of the senior staff directly. The president also reports that "all the board members have roots in Salingerville, if you scratch hard enough. . . . A lot are on [the board] because they want to come back and see their friends."

One board member living in Salingerville feels there is "not tremendous involvement in college affairs by local trustees," but she herself, even before joining the board, had "friendly relations" with members of the faculty and says she knows "more faculty members by name than anyone else on the board." She thinks it would be "chaotic if trustees nebbed [i.e., meddled] too much into affairs of the college," but she also feels that trustees are not asked to do enough. In particular, she thinks there should be "a total restructuring of the entire curriculum":

> And although the faculty thinks trustees don't know about these things,
> I would enjoy the input—although in the main it should be faculty
> ideas [that determine the outcome].

She is "badgered very seldom" by faculty members, except when someone is not granted tenure, and when this occurs she tells them, "It's a decision hard to make, and this is the judgment that was made." She implies that certain other members of the board would not be as restrained as she is and might want to reconsider the decision but "frankly, they don't know as much about [academic life and the faculty here] as I do." Besides, she adds: "I am not an instigator. I am prepared to listen, but I would not expose dirty linen in public."

Formally, the faculty has direct access to the board through a regularly scheduled meeting between the executive committee of the faculty and members of the board. There is also a committee of students that meets with trustees. It is variously reported by members of the Salinger board that the president is in attendance at these meetings and that he is not in attendance "because he says he doesn't want to come." The president mentions, however, the additional preparatory work that fell to his staff when these committee arrangements were originally established, and he clearly exercises some control over the agendas. One trustee reports that a good number of students turned out for a discussion of parietal rules, when the interested students "pulled in" other students and then parents, too. The board, he reports, eventually adopted regulations embodying 90 percent of the student recommendations, with a new member of the board, a woman, "leading the charge" on behalf of the students. On the whole, this trustee favors interchange between members of the board and faculty and students but thinks they should not be members of, or attend, board meetings because handling issues such as tenure would be "tricky." In his view the board should comport itself "like a town council." "That's good PR," he says, "and engenders greater respect for the college."

This trustee, a lawyer-lobbyist described as "not active" by the president, says he is "once a week, sometimes more" on the telephone to the vice-president for development, talks with the president by telephone once a month, and attends the Executive Committee meeting once a month, a trip of several hundred miles which he is able to combine with his business affairs. He obviously feels that trustees can have a significant impact on the college and spoke of his role in achieving tuition increases beyond the levels recommended to the board and of "redirecting the path" of the college's defense in a legal suit over tenure.

The chairman of the board, who works in the city one hour's drive east but maintains his home in Salingerville, calls the president "a good operator, a practical administrator" and says of the board that he "cannot recall a single instance of meddling." Of his own position vis-à-vis the president, he says,

> I run into the administration and faculty at social affairs. I know them very well. I try to create the impression that I'm not second-guessing the president. I try not to make statements about the college. People know I won't interfere in the day-to-day operation. I try to back the president.

The president, in turn, describes himself as a "power broker" and says the head of his board is a "strong chairman [who] keeps individual board members in check." The president is pleased on his own behalf at having "so far been successful in keeping the board out of curriculum." Because "finances have been of such major importance" in recent years, the board has been preoccupied by whether the college is "in the black," but, he implies, if board members had had the time, they might have gotten into curricular matters.

At present Dr. Griswold is thinking about the "problem of how we can use our board" and is concerned that there will be a "donnybrook" if the high level of participation of some board members were to be focused on curricular affairs. Trustees at Salinger are accustomed to addressing themselves to what one calls the "nitty-gritty"; it was a trustee, not an administrator, who prepared a sixty-page report on admissions which apparently persuaded the board that the potential for an enrollment crisis exists at the college. Indeed, the capacity of this board to tolerate appreciable involvement in the "nitty-gritty" is perhaps best illustrated by the chairman's description of the kind of trustee who makes the most significant contribution to the college's welfare:

> You want somebody [who will] leave home on a week night and say to some high school student, "Why don't you go to my school?"—a trustee who would travel continuously, [who] would furnish you the product you need. . . . It's not a job for an illustrious person; it's a job for a drudge.

He goes on to say, with some irony, that the ideal trustee "is a real dedicated housewife who will do nasty little jobs."

Commentary on Other Participatory Boards

As suggested by the example of Salinger College, trustees on a participatory board sometimes become involved in decisions that a corporate board would leave to the president's discretion. For example, the president of Cather College regularly experiences what he calls "interference in administration." Here he recounts a recent incident:

> The board thinks we should use five years out for planning, but two years is the latest in higher education planning, with speculation on the third year, which is what I've said all along.
>   And what I said to them was, I didn't think we needed an educational planner, but the accrediting agency recommends it, and they're coming next year.

And he concluded with some asperity, "You probably saw the new planning office. It's just down the hall." This president also finds it a minor but significant irritant to have to defer to the idiosyncracy of "a member of the Buildings and Grounds Committee who insists that the tennis courts be fixed—he plays tennis."

At Cummings College, a self-study of the board that solicited comments by "faculty selected by the faculty, all the top administrators, and other outside people," as well as board members, has revealed that the board "is far too much involved with operations and too little in policy." A "typical" example of overinvolvement in administration is described by the trustee who conducted the study:

> The board really wants to know what's going on. Last year the college had to come up with a solution to the computer problem: would we continue to use those at other institutions, or should we buy our own?
>
> The board received two-and-one-half inches of paper on this subject alone—and most of it was wordier than it need be.

This trustee goes on to say that the Cummings board has "invited" a high level of involvement, and many older trustees consider this kind of participatory oversight to be "their right and duty." These "veterans" have co-opted younger members who now say they have had "no opportunity to modify the style of the board." In this trustee's observation, the president has been "timid" about taking action without consulting the board, and the president "needs to provide leadership" to a board which is "floundering." The president, not surprisingly, has a different perspective. He observes that there is no way to make an "impermeable membrane" between the board and the campus, but he also feels that the Cummings board finds it difficult "to keep the constitutional boundary" and consequently tends to act as a "problem-solving senate."

Unlike the younger members at Cummings, those at Cather are eager to perpetuate the custom of "hands-on" participation. One younger Cather trustee, owner of a regional grocery chain, has been on the board for eight years but still recalls vividly his early feelings of bafflement:

> I was just plain frustrated when I first went on the board, just sitting there, getting the feel. I didn't make a lot of waves. I could see that decisions are made by a very few and brought to the board for them to say yes. What use could I be here, I wondered; I'm used to running a business and making decisions. Then [the past chairman of the board] and I had a discussion, and he said that if we accept trusteeship our obligation is for the long-term, on-going, positive development of the college, and that there are two kinds of trustees, those who are along for the ride and those who are concerned.
>
> Still I was frustrated because the board's concerns were too far removed from day-to-day operations. People like the [past] board chairman and [our member who is a real estate mogul] are not graduates, and those who went there have a different point of view.

As his comments imply, this trustee has not been content to limit his involvement to "concern." A member of what the president calls the "young men's network," this trustee, although not a member of the

Executive Committee, is on campus at least ten times during the year; as he says, if he were there just twice for the regular board meetings, it would be "frustrating." Sometimes he combines his college visits with business trips, and on such a stop he might meet with the college business manager or with the accountants who prepare the annual audit for the Audit Committee of which he is chairman. During these meetings he tries to "communicate: is the business manager happy and are the auditors? Are they working in an [auditing] framework that a businessman can understand?" Earlier he had been dissatisfied with the format of the auditor's reports and is very pleased that "now we have the auditor's report to the point that it's the way we operate in a business." On these visits, he often sees the fund-raising staff as well, and on homecoming weekends, "we know students, and my wife and I might go to a dormitory room."

Members of participatory boards do not conceive of the president as a CEO or powerful figure. He is a "practical administrator," a "communicator," of whom one Cather trustee says, "I always work through him, but everything doesn't clear with him." Presidents with participatory boards may find that "trustees as a group don't support the president," and if the trustees "listen to the forces turned against a good man, the guy can become," as the president of Cather warns, "a clerk." And indeed, the clerk's role in generating paper is suggested at Cummings when two-and-one-half inches of background material on a single issue is mailed to the board, presumably with the president's knowledge and assent.

The relatively ungoverned contact between a participatory board and faculty or students can complicate the president's dealings with board members. The president of Cummings speaks of a "lot of time, hard to quantify," which he spends in keeping his board "informed, reoriented, assuaged." The president of Cather speaks more bluntly. Although he says that the board "has caught on" to faculty members who are habitual complainers, he also admits, "I don't mind trustees being involved in policy, but when they listen to disgruntled faculty, it really ticks me off."

Not surprisingly, participatory boards view communication with campus constituencies as absolutely essential, a principle reflected in the Cummings chairman's enumeration of the main activities of his board: "managing fiscal affairs, . . . appointment and, if need be, termination of the president, . . . and in order to do these two, to communicate with the campus." But he cautions, "If you are constantly snooping, you're apt to undermine the president. It takes a little discretion as to how you handle this." Participatory board members say they are "apt to be in touch with senior tenured faculty" and "to know students on campus or to be related to them," but eliciting information from these sources is not an organized procedure.

One member of a participatory board observes that his board may take longer to do its business than others which operate differently:

> We're not interested in efficiency, we're interested in getting the right answer. It takes time to develop new information and new viewpoints. Most original thinkers look at things from many angles.

As this trustee thought back over his comments on the activities of the board, he speculated that the college might not need a president and that it could be "run very effectively by the top administrators and a board of the faculty."

A participatory board, like the corporate and ratifying boards, is likely to "rubber-stamp" the faculty's recommendations for tenure, and the assertion is made that the board "seldom gets into educational policy." Still, it appears that in practice the participatory board is more involved in the substance of educational policy than are the ratifying or corporate boards. For example, the board chairman at Cummings recalls a time when the president told the Academic Affairs Committee there was a move afoot among faculty members to abolish the senior-year seminar:

> The board was extremely unhappy. We didn't tell the president what to do, . . . but there was a strong indication by the board that [we would consider it a grievous mistake] if the senior seminars were given the ax. But we also said that we recognize that that's a faculty prerogative, and that we didn't want as a board to intervene with the educational program.
>
> And in the end, they came up with a compromise. I'm not sure another outcome was very likely, but on the other hand, [without our intervention] it might have been.

Another incident at Cummings demonstrates how difficult it can be for the member of a participatory board to decide in a particular instance what the limits of involvement should be in matters of educational policy. One trustee, through her attendance at meetings of the Academic Affairs Committee, knew that a new chairman for the fine arts department had been recruited several years previously with the charge to strengthen the department. This charge the new professor succeeded in implementing through great expenditure of time and effort; however, when the professor's name came up for tenure, it was evident that she had not pursued her scholarly specialty with the assiduousness required at Cummings. After a committee meeting at which the professor's status was discussed, the trustee attended a reception at the president's house, only to have the professor approach and ask if the question of her tenure had come up. The trustee, uncertain in her own mind about how to respond and feeling the president's eyes upon her from across the room, equivocated and resisted the impulse to say, "Go do your scholarship." The incident is still puzzling to the trustee, who says, "If I run into that professor again, I may try to tell her," and then she concludes, "but I don't have confidence in my judgment in this matter."

On the participatory board, the key issue is one of individual perspective—where on the continuum of involvement to position oneself. Members of participatory boards seem to find it difficult to be consistent because they tend to feel so intimately related to the institution—as alumni, through family connections, and through a conscientious desire to contribute—that each situation seems to be unique and to call for a special personal or board decision. Thus for the president, there is some certainty that on any issue arousing faculty or student opinion, a board member can be found who will champion that cause. This potential for finding a board champion may also exist at colleges with a corporate board, but the relative lack of informal relationships between faculty or students and board members makes it less likely that the cause and a potential champion will connect.

15 Commentary on the Three Operating Styles

The key to a board's operating style lies in the restraint displayed by its members, individually and as a group, in their relations with the president, the administrative staff, and other campus constituencies. Almost all trustees speak of the same basic responsibilities, particularly their fiduciary duties and their obligation to students, faculty, and alumni to perpetuate the liberal arts and secure excellence in higher education for the future. The way a board exercises these responsibilities, however, is a function of its particular culture and the norms of that culture as they are perceived by each board member.[1] Norms, which are rules of behavior, are dynamic and, in a small group such as a governing board, may rather quickly reflect changing ideas about commendable behavior as it is defined by individual members and by the group as a whole.[2]

The Culture of the Board

As we have seen, those having the most influence on the character of a board's norms are its chairman, the active members who actually spend time on board affairs, other key trustees, and the college president. But these individuals have to participate periodically in a group setting with the inactive members, and it is the sum of these influences that shapes a board's culture.

Trustees from different board room cultures tend to have varying ideas about appropriate behavior. A trustee on the ratifying board at Thoreau feels constrained in expressing his opinions about the kind of person the president ought to recruit as financial vice-president, so he limits himself to writing notes to the president—almost surreptitiously—between board meetings. In contrast, the chairman of the Student Affairs Committee at Cather is credited with having "gotten rid of" one dean of students and having recruited another, the norms of that participatory board sanctioning hands-on involvement by trustees in administrative matters. Occasionally a trustee will have personal values and expectations suggesting that he or she would feel more at home on a board with a different operating style. The note-writing Thoreau trustee, for example, would probably be more satisfied in a corporate environment where he might feel less defensive about making specific suggestions. There is also something of a mismatch on the corporate board at Twain, where two or three trustees are functioning in the participatory mode; partly to teach these irregulars how to be good corporate style trustees, Twain's board chairman is setting aside one mealtime during each trustee weekend when board members can be by themselves—no college staff, no spouses—to talk about current issues and how they might appropriately be pursued.

In the culture of the board room, one function of the operating style is to define the relationship between members and the president, and clearly, the more trustees are involved in day-to-day operations at the college, the less influence the president will have on their behavior and decision making. Thus at Poe, where the president is thought of as a chief executive, the trustee presenting a task force's recommendation knows that Poe's corporate board, though it insists on receiving background information, will rarely endorse any suggestion or change that does not have the president's support. In contrast, a trustee on Cather's participatory board speaks of "pushing" the president from time to time.

Occasionally a trustee, intentionally or out of naïveté, will violate the board's unspoken rule for relating to the president and other staff members, and this can be a serious trespass. For example, one trustee on Twain's corporate board recalls having a "unique relation" with the vice-president for development, with whom he began making plans and trying to set them into motion: "This can raise problems for the president. [The president] got annoyed at me that one time I got out ahead of him a little bit. It has made me careful [in my relations with staff members]."

Changes in Operating Style

And finally, the operating styles of boards tend to change over time, generally evolving from corporate to participatory and back. Cummings College is an example of this pattern of the swinging pendulum. Some years ago, the then-president of Cummings was a very strong chief executive who dominated the Executive Committee and expected the board to endorse that committee's recommendations. Two trustees on the board during that period feel that the present participatory mode at Cummings, which has existed for some years, can be explained as a simple reaction to that earlier very forceful president and his harsh corporate style. An evolution from the participatory mode presently ascendant at Cummings toward the corporate mode may well be in the offing, since the board's self-study has revealed considerable criticism of what some members apparently consider to be the excesses of the participatory mode there.

It is interesting that a change in operating style can be either revolutionary, as at Longfellow and Cummings several years ago, or evolutionary, as at Cummings and Thoreau at present. Trustees may act to encourage or impede such a change and may do so covertly or overtly, but it appears the impetus for a change in operating style often occurs by chance, the unplanned outcome of events which converge with the thoughts and feelings, often unarticulated, of board members. As the process of change gains momentum, a crisis occurs—an "explosion" over the budget in the Thoreau board room, questions about the nature of the president's leadership at Cummings—in which, as a by-product of the crisis issue, the legitimacy of current patterns of behavior is questioned. These patterns are then discarded abruptly or over time, but when the pendulum swings back again, the once-discarded patterns reappear.

16 Policy versus Administration

Whatever a board's operating style and degree of involvement in the day-to-day operation of the college, the rhetoric of the board room is that trustees "set policy" and rely on the president to administer policy. Egregious violations of this canon occur from time to time on every type of board, typically when one or two trustees pursue their pet interests. For example, an officer on the corporate board at Longfellow reports that

> [s]ome board members are too nit-picky and interfere in the prerogatives of the president and the staff: they want to be involved in scheduling economics classes. Raising questions is O.K., but their recommendations are usurping the president's authority. In the Student Life Committee, they're scheduling football games.

That scheduling economics classes and football games are administrative matters would be a judgment widely endorsed among trustees, but frequently the judgment about whether an issue is a policy or administrative item is not so easy to make, in part because the passage of time and a change in surrounding circumstances may alter the trustees' or the president's perspective.[1]

Difficulties in being specific about what policy consists of are not unique to higher education. As Richard M. Hodgetts and Max S. Wortman observe in *Administrative Policy:*

> When [business] executives are asked what "policy" means, they will often respond with innumerable definitions. . . . However, a commonly accepted definition is "a policy is a guide for carrying out action."[2]

Unfortunately, such a definition offers only limited practical and conceptual guidance. Even the most thoughtful of political scientists, sociologists, and organizational theorists have found it difficult to agree on refinements of the definition because, as Bertram Gross observes in *The Managing of Organizations,* "the making and execution of policy are inseparably intertwined. Genuine policy—as distinguished from meaningless generalizations—comes into being through the activities of the entire organization."[3] Gross goes on to say that what so-called policy-makers actually do in practice is to legitimate policies previously developed at lower levels, make "slight adjustments" in policy proposals, or occasionally choose among policy options.

In the face of these ambiguities, there are some matters that, by common consent, are recognized as policy issues appropriate to the college board room, among them approving the operating budget, approving faculty appointments and promotions, and deciding how to invest the endowment—the latter being the area in which trustees are most likely to originate policy as opposed to ratifying or slightly adjusting it. Although many other issues considered by trustees are difficult to classify, some might properly be described as administrative matters having significant implications for the college's public relations or for campus morale. While formal action is not taken on all of these quaisi-administrative items, a certain number are presented to the board in the form of requests for approval, such as a proposal from the Longfellow development office to establish an annual dinner for major donors. Then too, a problem that is clearly administrative, such as controlling vandalism on campus, may generate board discussion but no immediate action, although the issue may later take its place in the decision-making process. At Poe, vandalism is now being discussed by a trustee-student-faculty-administrative committee that will make policy-level recommendations to the board on the future of campus fraternities.

What seems to occur in the process of decision making is that the concepts of policy and administration emerge not as a dichotomy but as the two components of a spectrum. In such a context, the point on the spectrum at which an issue is decided grows out of a process that Paul Appleby, in his classic monograph *Policy and Administration,* described as a "subtle process of political evaluation," which includes "anticipation of popular reaction . . . a response to experience, convention, and precedent . . . [and] pressure from interests directly concerned."[4] Sensitivity to these forms of political agitation, especially when emanating from faculty and students, varies according to the governing board's operating style so that, as has been illustrated, the participatory board is more likely than the ratifying board to involve itself in issues on the administrative end of the policy-administrative spectrum.

Nowhere is the "subtle process of political evaluation" more evident than in the president's choice of items for the report he or she customarily makes at each meeting of the board or Executive Committee. The content of the report varies according to the board's operating style, the report to a participatory board generally being more detailed than that to a ratifying board. In any case, the report typically covers a variety of items from the policy-administrative spectrum, some of which are currently on the board agenda or will be in the future. Other topics are mentioned by the president not only to keep the board "informed," as presidents and trustees often say, but also to protect presidential interests: the president's report often serves as a counterweight to interpretations of campus events that trustees may receive through the student newspaper or from faculty acquaintances. Although a president usually does not intend for the board to become involved in all of the issues mentioned, the report may be perceived by trustees as inviting their comments and may have to be carefully worded if it is to signal clearly which issues the president considers appropriate for their further attention.

A Model of the Administrative Policy Structure

In the absence of an unambiguous definition of policy and administration that can be used to classify various trustee activities, it is useful to refer to the spectrumlike model developed by Hodgetts and Wortman to rationalize the policy-administrative process.[5] Their framework consists of six descending levels of generality including major policies, secondary policies, functional policies, minor policies, procedures and standard operating plans, and rules. Major policies resolve the broadest questions, such as whether a single sex college will become coeducational. Secondary policies cover somewhat narrower issues, such as whether a capital fund-raising campaign is to be undertaken or a faculty proposal for a department of business administration is to be approved. Functional policies, the third level, direct the day-to-day operation of the college and include approval of the annual operating budget. Minor policies include essentially procedural matters which are elevated in importance perhaps because they occur infrequently or are subjects of intense interest on campus; these might include selecting an architect for a new building or letting a food service contract for the dining halls. Procedures and standard operating plans govern ongoing operations such as the college's financial aid program. And rules, the sixth and most specific expression of policy, include dicta such as a regulation forbidding destruction of campus property. The various levels of the policy hierarchy are conceived of as mutually influencing, so that functional policies influence secondary ones and vice versa, rules have an effect on standard operating procedures, and so on.

That trustees are aware of the interactions among various levels of what is here termed the *policy structure* is often evident in their conversation. For example, a Twain trustee observes that there are "some places where operations and policy are very close," and for this reason, he feels, it is appropriate for board members "to be critical of the way decisions are implemented." As an illustration he hearkens back to the Twain board's decision to send one of its own members to take the president's place in difficult negotiations with the faculty over the cost-of-living component in their salary schedule. In terms of the six-level model of policy structure, the cost-of-living component for faculty salaries probably falls into the category of minor policy, although the issue certainly has implications for the operating budget, which is functional policy. At Twain, the issue also was resonant with the understanding among professors and trustees alike that Twain's faculty salaries are supposed to be competitive with Harvard's since both institutions draw from the same pool of top-flight academics; on this basis, a deterioration in the Twain salary schedule could result in a decline in the quality of faculty, and this possibility is a secondary policy issue. Perhaps it was the quality-of-faculty consideration which prompted the board to send one of its own members to the campus; in any case, although the two Twain trustees who mention this incident are aware that the immediate issue was perhaps administrative, they both feel strongly that their board's action was a legitimate expression of its policy-making function.

Similar in its potential for sending reverberations up and down a college's policy structure is a very different problem now developing at Salinger. According to a trustee familiar with the issue,

> [The question is], should members of a volunteer evangelical religious group be allowed on campus to act as dormitory proctors? The president called me and said another trustee is pushing for this. . . . One-half the funds [for the proctors' salaries] are provided by the religious group in exchange for being able to sponsor [voluntary] Bible study sessions on campus.

On an issue like this, which has implications for the character of the college and also has at least one trustee "pushing" for it, a president's phone calls for "guidance" will have the purpose not only of seeking substantive advice on a complex question but also of assessing the political landscape, the better to anticipate how the question might be received in the board room.

The Role of Committees in Policy Making

The governing board's committee structure is designed primarily to oversee the administrative departments, and since senior staff members produce the information considered by committees, the committee agendas tend to mirror the activities of the functional vice-presidents. Under these circumstances, it is not surprising that the policy issues coming to the committees are functional or minor policies. Illustrative of the bulk of recommendations for action made by standing committees to the board are the following:

—from the Property Committee at Salinger, a recommendation to give the president discretionary authority to purchase a $14,000 property;

—from the Executive-Finance Committee at Thoreau, a recommendation to approve an increase in health benefits for college employees and their dependents; and

—from the Committee on Educational Affairs at Longfellow, a recommendation to approve faculty sabbatical leaves, the recommendation being in the form of a request for approval of a memorandum from the academic dean reporting the action of a faculty committee.

In general, the time horizon on issues coming through committees is fairly short; it is longer on the relatively rare occasions when committees consider matters of secondary policy such as tenure ratios.

A secondary policy question, when it does arise, may come into focus as a corollary to an operational policy problem, as illustrated in a report on student fees made to the board by the Finance and Investments Committee at one of the colleges in this study. The report, written by the vice-president for finance, projects a decline in enrollment that will produce a shortfall in student fee revenues:

> [E]xpectations are that [the college's] enrollment will not decrease as much as the 8.6 percent projected nationally. To maintain current level programs in the next decade, the college must develop a $3 million reserve fund, and now a little over $1 million exists.

This report sets up the secondary policy question of whether to take extraordinary steps such as a capital campaign to raise monies for the reserve fund or to plan a pruning of programs in the expectation of an enrollment decline.

The process by which issues from the policy structure are brought to the board for action varies. On matters not directly affecting students and faculty, such as a capital fund-raising campaign, a proposal to proceed will come to the board in the form of a recommendation from the Development Committee, perhaps forwarded jointly with the Finance Committee. However, on matters influencing faculty and students more directly, particularly when the issues are apt to be controversial, most presidents in conjunction with their boards appoint an ad hoc, all-college committee which includes trustees, faculty members, students, and of course the senior administrator who collects data and prepares the report. In this fashion the board and the president, under the auspices of shared governance, formally involve important constituencies in the policy-making process.

These all-college committees play a significant role in the policy deliberations of the board. At Poe, for example, a trustee is chairman of an all-college task force that is probably going to recommend phasing out the fraternity system, a proposal far too controversial to delegate to the Committee on Educational Policy, where it would not be exposed to a broad range of campus opinion. At Thoreau, an all-college committee is responsible for making recommendations regarding long-range institutional planning.

Shared governance, as it is practiced through the all-college committee, significantly erodes the board's power to make policy. Unlike the board's standing committees, where students and faculty members are outsiders on what is basically a trustee committee, the all-college committee is a forum where trustees and students and faculty are on a more or less equal footing, and it is on this basis that the bargaining among participants takes place. As a result, the position the board finds itself in upon receiving the committee's report is identical to its position when it receives the recommendations of a presidential search committee. That is, in endorsing the report of an all-college committee, trustees may find they are supporting recommendations which do not conform to their own preferences, whereas if they withhold endorsement in whole or in part, they may appear to be repudiating their own representatives and to be rejecting advice they asked for in the first place.

Happenstance in Policy Making

Not all policy issues can be anticipated, and not always are the ramifications of a particular incident recognized by the participants in the rush of events. For example, one president recalls "a big hassle" over how to collect student dues for the campus chapter of a national student organization. The students wanted to use a refundable mechanism, whereby they would pay dues along with tuition but might later request a refund, while the administration had decided to use a negative checkoff whereby the students could avoid paying dues with tuition by checking off "no." The board, which learned of the dues question first through the student newspaper and later through the student-trustee liaison committee, concluded that the college should not collect funds for any organization for which it did not hire and control the personnel—an issue of operating policy. In the course of these deliberations, however, the board's Executive Committee did not give much thought to deciding whether the dues question was a policy or administrative issue. The trustees apparently acted instead on the principle that "if we see something potent or damaging, and if we have time, we will deal with it."

At another college, one trustee asserts that "policy is made by accident." He is not speaking of unusual situations in which the board is caught by surprise—as the trustees described above were caught unawares by the dues checkoff issue—but of systematic lapses in policy formulation and approval in the areas of curriculum, faculty personnel, and admissions. He says that the curriculum at his college is shaped by the accident of student demand and that "what departments the college should have are determined by present uses, by students and faculty, and not by thought [undertaken] in advance." In the area of faculty affairs, he describes a lapse in which a policy was never formally approved by the board:

> A current distressed area results from a faculty member being permitted and then denied permission [by a faculty-administration committee] to do classified research. A policy was developed by the faculty and administration and we [the board] were told about the policy [by the president], but the board didn't object when the policy never came up for approval. So nobody can be held accountable. The president can't be held accountable, and now 140 faculty are involved.

And in admissions, he does not feel it appropriate for the admissions staff and the admissions committee to be left with the responsibility for making a minor policy decision that has major implications for alumni relations and fund raising:

> A director of admissions ought to know whether there are any policy limitations imposed. There was a time when [the administration] was told that it was a board policy that we must admit all qualified sons and daughters of alumni. It's entirely proper for a board to make such a rule and wrong for the decision to be made by anyone except the board.

And the trustee concludes by saying that "most of these policy areas should be initiated by the president."

The President and Policy Making

The way presidents handle the policy structure with their boards seems less a function of certainty about what a policy issue really is than a defensive tactic for dealing with the board's operating style. Thus a president with a participatory board will find that if the board is to remain satisfied, it must become involved in issues which a corporate board might consider administrative. For example, the minutes of a typical Executive Committee meeting at Frost College might show the committee's action in approving faculty appointments and student fees, as well as action to establish a restricted endowment fund. At Salinger College, which has a participatory board, the Executive Committee agenda would include not only those items but also requests for approval to loan a $45,000 art work to a museum and to sell the bowling machines in the student center. And as has been indicated, varying levels of detail are also reflected in the presidents' reports to the board, so that while a corporate board's president will confine comments on student life to a review of the progress of a task force, a participatory board's president will comment specifically on details related to sororities, fraternities, and the performance of a student musical group. In other words, when a president decides, by instinct or design, how far down the policy structure to involve and inform the board, he or she is making a political judgment about the board's operating style and about how much information need be given and in what form to maintain the board's confidence and goodwill.

Implementation in a Collegiate Setting

Although governing boards tend to be defensive about any accusation that they are "meddling" in administration, many members are frank in admitting their interest in the impact on campus of the president's style of administering; these trustees are convinced that how policy is implemented is very important to its attainment. And it is true that what is known about the sociology of organizations suggests that style of behavior may be more important in the success of a college presidency than it is in a business presidency. As Amitai Etzioni has demonstrated, an educational organization differs from a business organization in the importance attached by its members to symbols, particularly symbols of prestige, esteem, love, and acceptance.[6] On the small college campus many of these intangible rewards are in the hands of the president, who may be called upon at any time to deal with the symbolic as well as operational value of, for example, a faculty salary schedule equivalent to Harvard's.

Especially if a president has few opportunities personally to inform, educate, and persuade individual faculty members and students, the capacity to appeal to the ideals of academic life and to interpret its symbols effectively can be useful. Yet few trustees seem to have thought systematically about how the board might create an atmosphere that would encourage the president to capitalize upon opportunities for symbolic leadership. Nor do trustees always seem to recognize that the campus's sensitivity to symbols may invest a board's public reversal of the president's decision, however justified, with a larger significance than it had in the board room; such actions may also subtly erode the willingness of the faculty and students to respond to presidential leadership. As one president remarked after the board had rather abruptly and publicly reversed his decision on collecting dues for a national student organization, "Are the students supposed to come to us [the administration] or the board?"

IV Concluding Observations

17 The Impact of the Board upon the College

This study began with two questions, What do trustees actually do, and How do their activities affect the college? Certainly a study purporting to offer a truly comprehensive answer would be much larger than this one and would necessarily include interviews with faculty members, alumni, students, and senior administrators. Still, on the basis of conversations with presidents and members of the board, generalizations can be made which I believe will be of some use to trustees, presidents, and others who are concerned about the potential and limitations of the governing board as an institutional resource.

To review briefly, what has emerged is the proposition that although the structure of governing boards is similar from one college to another, the process of oversight is carried out by trustees in one of three operating styles—identified as ratifying, corporate, and participatory—which embrace the board's informal decision-making processes and its members' relationships with the president, faculty, and student body. As a discrete organizational subunit, the board functions within a set of constraints consonant with its status as a volunteer group but unique within the collegiate organization. In particular, since trustees do not participate in the day-to-day operations of the college, they are dependent upon others for information, and how a board chooses to solicit and receive such information is a central feature of its operating style. We have also seen that governing boards, like other bureaucratically structured volunteer groups, function as oligarchies, dominated in the collegiate instance by the chairman and key trustees. All of these factors, in combination with the individual members' attitudes and experiences, influence the nature of the board's impact upon the college.

Impact upon the Presidency

A significant and altogether unintended influence of the governing board has been to diminish the office of the presidency through neglect of its expressive and honorific aspects. In the trustees' expectations of the college president, bureaucratic means seem to predominate over the intellectual and heroic ends of educational leadership, and the result has been an erosion of the leadership potential inhering in the office. This lowering of expectations may begin with the presidential search, when the candidate selected may not be the trustees' first choice; in any event, the trustees will expect the new president to demonstrate the political skills necessary to cope with the competing interests of the college's various constituencies while ensuring that important administrative activities and proposed programs are documented on paper and circulated to the board. These expectations may simply reflect a socioeconomic environment that encourages trustees to emphasize administrative adroitness more than a continuing intellectual engagement with what Matthew Arnold once called "the best that is known and thought in the world," but as a result, neither an interest in educational innovation nor a deeply felt concern for intellectual values is likely to be strongly reinforced by the board. It is not surprising, therefore, that only a few trustees speak of expanding the scope of the presidency beyond the coordination of bureaucratic paper work and the mediation of conflicting claims.

What seems to have happened is that the relationship between the board and the president often proceeds on the basis, unspoken and unacknowledged, that no single president is likely to be able to make a critical difference in advancing the institution's welfare. Assuming it unlikely that any particular president can make much difference, governing boards tend to support most readily the president who succeeds not only in avoiding significant antagonism, particularly from the faculty, but also in functioning competently as a coordinator of vice-presidential specialists perceived to be doing the substantive work of the college.[1] These limitations on the presidency are not imposed on a naïve and victimized incumbent; rather, each president seems to have developed an equation for surviving the hazards of shared governance under highly politicized conditions. In this environment, some presidents have moments when they see themselves as journeymen and transients somewhat at the mercy of a governing board overly responsive to faculty and student complaints.

Presidents are continually on their guard in their relationship with the board. They are especially wary of the tendency of board members individually and collectively to "interfere" in the day-to-day administration of the college, and at heart, most presidents, to a greater or lesser extent, would prefer, in the words of the president of Twain, "that the board stand at a somewhat greater distance." Yet on the whole, a president's feelings of defensiveness seem to be balanced by an appreciation of the expertise and advice available to the college by virtue of the skills and experience of various board members. The president of Melville, for example, values a trustee who chooses an area of interest and pursues it in a measured, consistent manner over a period of time. The presidents of Cummings and Salinger, respectively, speak of the benefit to themselves and their boards' decision-making processes of "a variety of backgrounds . . . and the judgments they bring to bear" and of a "perspective different from the administration." Several presidents, like the president of Thoreau who says the board "protects the president from making stupid mistakes," find it helpful to consult various trustee "experts" as a "sounding board" for their own thinking. The president of Cummings observes that "the president needs to define his thinking by talking [with trustees]," and the president of Poe speaks to the mutuality of influence that can exist between a board and a president when he says, "They influence me as much as I influence them."

When trustees speak of the influence they have on the president, a word that comes to their minds is "support." Their thinking is on two tracks. On the one hand, because the president is their agent on campus, they feel organizationally responsible for supporting him or her; at the same time, many trustees are personally motivated to support the president simply because they sympathize and empathize with the person who is tackling a job they believe to be one of society's most challenging. On the other hand, when a trustee's personal judgment on a given issue is at variance with the president's action, the trustee's support becomes problematic, and in these instances, the trustee's decision about whether to "back" the president is strongly influenced by the board's operating style. Trustees on a ratifying board are likely to give strong support with few questions asked, those on a corporate board to give public support while asking a good many searching questions of the president privately and in the board room, and those on a participatory board to express openly their own personal views if queried by faculty or students. In other words, the strength of the obligation a board member feels to support a president varies according to the board's operating style.

Impact upon the Administrative Departments

It is difficult to assess the influence of the governing board on the activities of the administrative departments in spite of the substantial amount of time that trustees devote to their oversight. The committee system provides a forum for trustees to pursue specific issues and an opportunity for them to contribute a certain amount of free labor, as in the case of the Salinger trustee who had the staff at his own office prepare an exhaustive report on admissions. On the whole, however, many of the initiatives for which trustees take credit appear to have existed in embryonic form within the administration or to have had such wide currency that trustees and senior staff may have picked up on an idea almost simultaneously. Even so, the part trustees play by applauding progress and serving as an audience for senior administrators probably has a constructive influence on the quality of results and the speed with which projects are completed.

Impact upon the Educational Program

Trustees' influence on the content of the educational program appears to be negligible, and presidents can be seen as guardians of the curriculum who expend considerable energy forestalling incursions by the board into this area. However, considering the conventional wisdom that board members prefer to concentrate almost exclusively on "green grass, buildings, and tangible things," the interest that a number of them express in the liberal arts as an educational ideal and in the content of the curriculum is unexpected.

Impact upon Financial Condition

At variance with the board's presumed leadership in fund raising is the assertion by a number of trustees that the president is the chief fund-raiser. Their view is based, apparently, on the president's responsibility to cultivate prospective donors (some of whom may be board members), often over a long period, and ultimately to put the hard question, "Will you give . . . ?" A trustee, in contrast, may only occasionally make a key, and presumably effortless, telephone call to provide the president with entrée. Still, without that telephone call, the president might not be able to get beyond the door to make the presentation. It appears also that some presidents, through their own professional networks, have contacts at foundations which prove more fruitful than the connections provided by the board. However, foundation gifts often require some form of financial leadership, so that without a "good giving board," as one president puts it, a president's contacts may yield little. All things considered, the president is perhaps most accurately represented not as the chief fund-raiser, but as the board's full partner in a joint endeavor.

As might be expected, most trustees say that assuring the "financial integrity" of the college is as important as their responsibility for hiring and firing the president, and in an era of uncertain enrollment trends and fluctuating interest rates, the way boards go about trying to ensure financial stability is an object lesson in how very much easier it is to be rich. One elite institution in this study has just completed an enormously successful capital campaign, and another prestigious, well-endowed college is beginning a campaign with great confidence. But at a less prestigious and less academically selective institution, the choice the trustees have faced is between borrowing money at high interest to construct a new building and then incurring substantially increased operating costs or doing nothing and hoping that, in a competitive admissions environment, a less attractive physical plant will not discourage already scarce applicants. Trustees of poorly endowed, middle-rank institutions frequently encounter this kind of decision, and for these colleges, the margin for error in judgment is narrow indeed.

Impact upon Policy

The presumed policy-making role of the board, this study suggests, is at the very least a misnomer. In practice, issues of policy and administration are not always easy to distinguish, and policy implications can be extrapolated from almost any action. Consequently, the internal politics of the institution, rather than the objective importance of an issue, may determine whether a decision is referred to the board. Although the board's policy-making role has long been circumscribed by the tradition of sharing authority with other constituencies, particularly the faculty, it has been subtly eroded more recently by the prevalence of the ad hoc, all-college committee which is frequently appointed to advise the board. After representatives of the trustees, students, and faculty have devoted hours to discussions and bargaining from their varied points of view, the board may find it difficult to do anything other than adopt the committee's recommendations, whether or not board members wholeheartedly agree with them. In these circumstances, it is difficult even for board members themselves to sustain the illusion that they actually "make" policy; in defining their policy role, they imply that the board reviews and approves policy, as distinguished from developing it. They speak of the board's impact on the college as "seeing that there is a policy." Within this framework, the board is less a policy-maker than a policy-participant with substantial powers to reject, review, and modify.

Another factor reducing the board's influence on policy is the trustees' immersion in the ongoing administrative programs of the functional departments. This preoccupation may put the board in the position of failing to see the proverbial forest for the trees and may explain why the one organizational subunit with an institution-wide perspective does not seem to utilize fully its unique capacity for initiating broad policy questions. Perhaps the seductiveness of paperwork for trustees and their devotion to operations reflect an information-rich society and the work habits of executives and professionals accustomed to responding to briefing memos and the day-to-day vicissitudes of organizational life. If so, these proclivities are reinforced by trustees' perceptions of their own success; most consider their success self-made and associate their own achievements with thinking clearly about concrete issues and having the better idea. In my view, these attitudes and experiences strongly dispose board members to place a high value on the functional policies and procedures of various administrative departments and to devote substantial time to them. Yet presumably it is from a strategic perspective—a broader outlook which transcends the functional areas—that productive thinking will have to be done if colleges are to thrive—and for some, survive—in an uncertain economic, regulatory, and demograpic environment.[2]

The Board as an Institutional Resource

It seems clear that the energies and talents of governing boards are in some measure misdirected and that, as a result, some of their potential value to the college is not being realized. While it is true, as one trustee cautions, that boards are not supposed to engage in "supermanagement," this is exactly what oversight tends to become. In effect, college trustees become senior partners to the vice-presidents, and the day-to-day problems of the functional areas become the primary focus of the energies and interests of the majority of active board members. This focus is not necessarily bad in itself, except that it tends to become a substitute for hard thinking from an institution-wide perspective, and this perspective is the unique preserve of the governing board.

Active board members bring to their trustee pursuits intelligence and broad experience. They are willing to devote substantial amounts of time to the college, and their vision of what they can do for the institution is often quite specific and operational—they are proud of the expertise they can offer. As a consequence, few are likely to suggest that the best thing they might do during their weekends on campus is to spend more time talking together in an organized fashion about the imponderables of the future; a "good working board" simply does not sit around refining its thinking in conversation that in the short term leads to nothing—no motion, no committee meeting, and maybe not even a background paper to be prepared by a vice-president or dean. Similarly, the trustees' well-meaning willingness to "work" tends to truncate the board's exposure to the depth and breadth of the president's thinking, since much of his or her conversation in the board room consists of an itemized, half-hour report and brief replies to questions. Yet, if the usual expectations of board activity could be shed, it might seem quite sensible to spend a substantial amount of time simply listening to the president expand upon his or her views, relying on the questions and discussions that follow to help refine the president's thinking while he or she is refining the board's.

Many of today's trustees are sensitive to the accusation that their predecessors were "rubber stamps," and they are proud that the same cannot be said of them. Instead, these men and women of goodwill, eager to play a significant role in securing the college's welfare, find themselves taking the part of expert consultants. It is a role that produces tangible outcomes and, trustees believe, legitimates the board as a contributing participant in the collegiate organization. But it is a role that often leaves largely unrealized the strategic and developmental perspectives a governing board is uniquely able to foster.

18 Some Implication for Theory and Practice

Although the vagaries and supposed imperfections in human behavior seem universally to be of considerable interest, our patience is often taxed by prescriptions for improvement that may be quite irksome, involving as they do assumptions with which we may not agree and recommendations for changes in behavior that may seem altogether too troublesome or unrealistic. These considerations have led me to withhold for a short final chapter an analysis of how trusteeship has been weakened as it has become removed from its theoretical underpinnings. I also suggest that a reconsideration of the theory underlying lay trusteeship implies an important change in present practice which will have the result of making governing boards more effective.

From the perspective of the institution, the governing board's focus on day-to-day operations reduces its impact on broad policy, while from the perspective of the society at large, the board's role as institutional advocate minimizes its usefulness as an instrument of the public interest. In practice, few private college trustees think of themselves as performing a civic act, although governing boards were originally, as they still are, accountable to the state which charters them. And although a case can be made that members of private college boards are less pressed by the contemporary dilemmas of accountability than are members of public boards, the basic ambivalence of the role remains: Is the trustee responsible to the college or to the public beyond the campus gates? Focusing on this question and on the issues following from it is one way, I believe, that governing boards can increase their impact upon the college to the benefit not only of the institution but also of society.

Providing for the Public Interest

The concept of a "public interest" which transcends "special interests" and individual preference, and to which institutions and individuals are answerable, lies at the heart of democratic theories of government. Beginning with Plato, the concept has been implicit in the search for forms of government conducive to responsible decision making, and for the seventeenth-century American colonists, the solution to this basic question of political philosophy included the separation of the church from the state and the use of the corporation as an intervening structure between the individual and the state. This formula, as interpreted in the founding of the earliest American colleges, led to an autonomous governing board with full authority over the institution but answerable to the state *pro publico bono*.[1] Subsequently, in 1819, limits on the power of the state over a college were set by Chief Justice John Marshall in his opinion in the Dartmouth College case, which established the "autonomy" of private colleges, even though the element of accountability remained.

Today, few trustees conceive of their role as a form of public responsibility; only lawyer trustees are apt to point out that boards are legally accountable to the state in which they are chartered. In fact, when asked to whom a college board is accountable, the majority of trustees say they are accountable to themselves, but many immediately qualify that assertion by referring to what they call a "moral" accountability to, as a Thoreau trustee puts it, "everyone that is touched by decisions that the board makes." Among this constituency, some groups are more important than others, and most trustees feel an ongoing sense of primary responsibility toward members of the faculty and present students. Secondarily, they are concerned about maintaining traditions which are important to the alumni and to the character of the college, such as senior year seminars or an outstanding athletic program. Then, in a rather generalized way, some trustees feel accountable to the public at large in the sense that private higher education is recognized as performing a public function. Overall, as this ordering of preferences suggests, trustees are ambivalent about how much to leaven their advocacy of the institution and its present employees and students with considerations of a broader nature.

That private college trustees see themselves principally as advocates of the institution is an example of a dynamic identified elsewhere by political scientists; according to this research, nonprofessional groups that oversee professionalized agencies do not represent the public interest effectively over the long term because they tend to become captive to the narrow concerns of the agency's professionals, whose interests they begin to defend.[2] In their exemplification of this tendency, the small college board is like the United States Congress where, through the standing committee system, members (encouraged and often led by their staffs) become deeply involved in administrative detail and the daily operations of the federal bureaucracy and become advocates of their particular legislative fiefdoms rather than impartial overseers.

In the collegiate sector, this dynamic has become so well recognized that except in litigation, private college boards have rarely been viewed as accountable for lapses in social responsibility within the organizations they theoretically govern. Federal regulators, for example, have customarily by-passed the governing board and have dealt directly with the college administration in requiring the institution to accommodate larger numbers of women, minorities, or the handicapped both in the student body and among the faculty and staff. Only with respect to the practice of investing in companies with holdings in South Africa—an instance where the board itself is viewed as the operating unit through its Investment Committee—has the board in recent times been called to account on an issue of social responsibility,[3] and in this case the objections have been raised by students and faculty, not by a governmental body. Otherwise, as the active trustees have turned inward toward the institution to legitimate their roles, they have tended to undermine rather than reinforce their own authority and, by default, to increase rather than forestall the diffusion of power to agencies external to the campus.

Toward More Effective Governance

The question remaining is how governing boards in higher education, particularly private college boards, will respond to issues of the public interest during the period of declining enrollment and increasing financial pressure forecast for institutions in many parts of the country. If boards remain institutional advocates only, they may invite by default further government regulation or some other form of legislative or judicial intervention.

In my view what is required, if the board is to take the initiative in responding to changing economic, social, and political conditions, is nothing more or less than the restructuring of the board's committee system. This change must be made if the board is to direct its attention to issues of the public interest and if, as a corollary to those concerns, the board is to carry out its policy role, broadly conceived. In particular, some standing committees need to be abolished and the meeting times of those which remain reduced so that the "work" of the board can be focused on the themes arising when the relationship between the college and society is examined. Ad hoc committees need to be appointed to meet over the course of one to three years to discuss topics such as interinstitutional cooperation; interinstitutional competition; vocational opportunities for liberal arts graduates; the effect of state, federal, and institutional aid programs on enrollment; the meaning of the "value-added" concept in higher education; and the role of the undergraduate college in lifelong learning. Each of these topics would draw upon background information from various of the college's functional departments and might include discussions with representative faculty members and students. The president, whose role has heretofore been diminished by the bureaucratic routines of administrative oversight, would be a key intellectual figure in these deliberations that bear, after all, on the essence of institutional leadership.

Attention to the public interest would force trustees to adopt a broad, policy-level perspective, and from this vantage point the governing board might begin to position itself as a more valuable participant in important institutional decisions. Freed from the strait jacket of functional committee agendas, board members would have time to define and discuss major issues and, when appropriate, would be in a position to make a considered choice about how the board's role as an advocate of the institution properly balances with the public welfare in situations where the interests of the public and the college are inconsistent. If, for example, a college's financial viability for the coming four years were to be in doubt, would trustees decide that students and prospective students should be informed of this possibility? Or would they decide to make no announcement for fear of scaring away the very students whose presence would be required to maintain financial viability? These kinds of circumstances, anticipated over the next decade, will test board members' moral and civic virtue.

Of course, inherent in any idea for reform is the possibility of new distortions and unexpected consequences, and a board self-consciously cloaked in the mantle of the public interest would probably be no exception, as these observations of David Riesman suggest:

> Would [this idea] lead to the board's meeting being dominated by those with advocacy experience in what they themselves deem to be public interest causes? Rather than educate members of the board who have had less involvement with civic virtue, it might disfranchise them.[4]

And indeed, it would be a most unfortunate outcome of "reform" if moral posturing were to be substituted for operational expertise as the *sine qua non* of trustee decision making! As a practical matter, therefore, it may be wise for trustees and the president simply to agree among themselves to shift the board's attention away from day-to-day operations and toward a process of strategic thinking and planning that takes into account the institution's responsibility to the commonweal. Trustees themselves are not responsible for the substance of these plans—although some will be able to contribute useful ideas—but they are responsible for seeing that this kind of thinking is accomplished. To this end, the increased use of ad hoc committees devoted to broad policy issues would be a useful mechanism.

Appendix I: Methodology

At the outset of this study in the early 1980s, it was important to identify a population of private, four-year liberal arts colleges sufficiently homogeneous to permit meaningful generalization. Since my preference was to build on previous research by selecting a population based on established typologies of higher education institutions, I began by reviewing the typologies used by the National Center for Education Statistics, the American Council on Education, the Carnegie Council on Policy Studies in Higher Education, and Baldridge et al.[1] It then appeared that out of a total universe of slightly more than 3,000 postsecondary institutions, there are, according to Carnegie, 572 private liberal arts colleges. The ACE typology, which categorizes on the basis of institutional control, includes 1,250 private, four-year accredited institutions, of which 256 are Roman Catholic, 436 are controlled by some other sectarian group, and 554 are nonsectarian. None of the typologies reviewed includes a separate stratum for nonsectarian private colleges with a liberal arts curriculum.

Working from the ACE typology, I excluded sectarian institutions, since the problem of determining which variations in trustee behavior are due to sectarian influence would have added a needless intervening variable to the study. On the same basis predominantly black and single-sex institutions were excluded. Then, to eliminate variations in findings attributable to large size and administrative complexity, institutions with more than 2,500 full-time equivalent students were excluded, as well as those offering degrees other than the baccalaureate and master's. Finally, I went through the *Education Directory, Colleges and Universities*, published by the National Center for Education Statistics, and enumerated every institution that falls within the parameters described above. In the course of this enumeration, I eliminated additional institutions that, although listed as "independent, nonprofit" in the *Education Directory*, had members of religious orders in chief administrative positions.[2] The resulting total was 184 private, nonsectarian liberal arts colleges.

One alternative at that point would have been to draw a random sample from the population of 184, but I was concerned about repeating an undesirable outcome of random sampling that had occurred in the Davis and Batchelor survey of trustees.[3] Their original random sample produced so many institutions of "low visibility" that the sponsoring agency, the Association of Governing Boards of Universities and Colleges, insisted on adding institutions which would make the sample seem more representative and give the study more credibility.

As an alternative to random sampling, I opted for a judgment sample of ten colleges that, in addition to meeting the criteria outlined above, seemed to me to be varied enough in selectivity, prestige, age, and location to assure valid conclusions. The colleges thus selected are located in four states, and all are single-campus, residential institutions that are private, nonsectarian, regionally accredited, non-profit, coeducational, and do not have predominantly black student bodies. All have fewer than 2,500 full-time equivalent students and confer the baccalaureate degree, with some conferring the master's as well. In academic selectivity, according to the six-category rating scale used in *Barron's Profiles of American Colleges*, Twelfth Edition, two rank in the fourth category, four in the third category, and four in the first or second categories.[4]

Just as these institutions as a group represent a higher level of academic selectivity than the universe of institutions from which they were drawn, so too is this sample overrepresentative of colleges founded in the last half of the eighteenth century.[5] Four institutions in this sample (40 percent) were founded between 1751 and 1800, whereas, of private institutions still extant, only 1.5 percent were founded during that period. Two colleges (20 percent) were founded between 1801 and 1850, compared with 12 percent nationally, and three (33 percent) were founded between 1851 and 1900, just about equivalent to the national statistic of 36 percent. One college (10 percent) was founded between 1900 and 1950, compared with 34 percent nationally. It may be that longevity and selectivity are proxies for a mix of variables not considered, such as size of the endowment, expertise of the administration, quality of the faculty, and good luck. In any case, I felt that findings based on a sample somewhat weighted in favor of the best and better and more venerable of the nation's colleges would be more persuasive than would results based on a more rigidly representative grouping.

Once the colleges were selected, I wrote to each president explaining the purpose of the study and asking if I might interview him. When the president agreed to participate, I then asked if I might arrange additional interviews by writing directly to the chairman of the board of trustees, the chairman of a standing committee, and two other board members the president might suggest who were not officers or committee chairmen. The result was a group of trustees whose occupational and personal characteristics, as described in the introduction, vary substantially from the national average for all private college boards.[6]

Each president was interviewed in his office and each trustee in his or her home or office, as he or she might prefer. The conversations generally lasted between one and two hours, and I took notes by hand, discarding the alternative of a tape recorder because it seemed cumbersome to me, and I feared that even the smallest machine might seem intrusive to the interviewees. The conversations were conducted with the understanding that the identity of individual trustees and their institutions would be disguised. As I mention in the introduction, disguise has serious consequences in research because it lessens the public accountability that can be brought to bear on the researcher; the readers of these pages, except for the principals, who will of course recognize themselves and their own institutions, will not be able to compare the impressions presented here with their own perception of the governing boards at these colleges. Still, disguise seemed imperative in a study that tries to get behind formalities and façades; few trustees or presidents would want to put their institution in a bad light by describing practices which might merit criticism.

The method of disguise used here has involved withholding the exact dates of events, changing the name of the president and certain particulars of his educational background and experience, changing the geographic location of each college and characteristics of its physical plant, and withholding the names of trustees and altering their occupations when their titles might identify them to a broad range of friends and business colleagues. In addition, I have given each college a false name and, except where a confidence would be betrayed, have attributed the comments of its president and trustees to the falsely named institution.

Appendix II:
Thumbnail Sketche
of Colleges and
Trustees
in the Study

Cather College

Cather College is located in the rural foothills of some eastern mountains. As on many college campuses, the buildings are a mix of the new with the old, but the effect at Cather is somewhat ragtag, as if the place had been designed to accommodate poor relations, while the sons and daughters of the more prosperous branch of the family went elsewhere. As the chairman of the board remarks:

No one has ever heard of the name. "What? Where is that?" they say. And of course there's an inferiority feeling all of us have, and so we are determined to make the college well known.

The president of the college, Dr. Jacob Alexander, is in his late fifties and has been at Cather for five years. This is his third small college presidency, and it is said that he came to Cather because he wanted to return to the East and "to the liberal arts." He has built a summer home on Cape Cod, and it is expected that he will retire there in a few years.

The college accepts three of every four students who apply, and median SAT scores fall in the low 500s; 40 percent of the graduates go on for further study. Three-quarters of the students are from within the state.

The chairman of the Cather board is a corporate vice-president of a Fortune 500 company. An alumnus in his early sixties, he says he is "still one of the younger members of the Cather board." Two members of his family have been presidents of the college, and another relative is presently on the faculty.

A younger Cather trustee, in his mid forties, is also an alumnus and is president of a family-owned business, a regional stockbrokerage. Both his grandfather and grandmother were members of the board, and his father was chairman of the board.

Another young Cather trustee, class of '57, owns a regional grocery chain. He was "frustrated" when he first went on the board because its concerns seemed so far removed from day-to-day operations, while he was accustomed to "running a business and making decisions."

A committee chairman, class of '34, has been on the board for well over twenty years. He lives within a short drive of the campus and has observed three Cather presidents from that vantage point. He owned and operated a retail business from which he is now retired.

Cummings College

The heart of the Cummings College campus is a cluster of classroom buildings and dormitories adjacent to the older residential area of a prosperous town. The college accepts about 45 percent of those who apply, and median SAT scores for entering freshmen exceed 575. Attrition, at 15 percent over four years, is low, and about 70 percent of the students pursue advanced studies following graduation.

The president of the college, Dr. Daniel Allbritten, received his baccalaureate and doctor's degrees at elite institutions and is an archeologist with a special interest in Central and South America. This is his seventh year in office.

The chairman of the board, an alumnus, is a retired professor and former department head at a private university. He is intrigued by the challenges, time and again, of bringing to a point of amicable agreement the experienced and independent-minded individuals who make up the Cummings board.

A senior trustee, also an alumnus, is a retired banker who has been on the board for over fifteen years and lives just a few miles from the college. He has come to the conclusion that the faculty and the president on a college campus are "natural adversaries."

One of the younger members of the board graduated in the late 1960s and is now an educational administrator. She is chairman of the Committee on Academic Affairs and has foregone other volunteer activities in order to attend conscientiously to the business of the Cummings board.

A fourth board member, elected just a year ago after being nominated by the alumni association, is a retired college president and is also trustee of another private college. On the basis of his background and experiences, he believes that "boards are very different in their attitudes toward themselves."

Faulkner College

With its classrooms and dormitories spread across an open campus, Faulkner College is within walking distance of the commercial district of a small town. The college accepts less than one-third of its applicants, and 80 percent of the enrolled students come from out-of-state. Median SAT scores for entering freshmen exceed 575, and 75 percent of graduates go on for further study.

The president of the college, now forty-two, was educated at an elite men's college and, after receiving a law degree, earned his doctorate in philosophy. Prior to assuming the presidency two years ago, he was academic dean at a respected liberal arts college.

The chairman of the board, a lawyer, practices with a leading urban firm and is active behind the scenes in state politics. He enjoys "contact with the faculty and administration and of course the board members," and he recalls missing associations with the college when he lived abroad some years ago. He is an alumnus.

The vice-chairman of the board is now retired from law practice with a prominent metropolitan firm and divides his time between an apartment in the city and a summer home near the campus. An alumnus of the college, he says with humorous self-deprecation that he was appointed to the board many years ago through the efforts of a clergyman who was looking for a favor in return.

The youngest trustee on the board is twenty-seven and was appointed to the board after serving as president of the college's largest alumni club. With a job as an elementary school counselor and family responsibilities as well, she is less able than in the past to keep abreast of college affairs.

A Faulkner graduate from the mid 1960s is now a law professor and describes himself as outspoken during board meetings. Interested in the interplay between human character and social institutions, he believes that events can be significantly influenced by the individual personality.

Frost College

Frost College, its buildings connected by pathways criss-crossing a rolling campus, is located in a small city. The college accepts less than one-half of its applicants, and median SAT scores for freshmen exceed 575. Fifty percent of graduates pursue further study, with 10 percent entering law school.

The president of the college, Dr. Robert Roberts, was once an editor and later a university administrator. He came to the Frost presidency over fifteen years ago and has been in office long enough to see many of his presidential colleagues come and go and to be distinguished by his own staying power.

The chairman of the board is soon to retire from his position as a senior operating officer in a Fortune 500 conglomerate. A dedicated alumnus, he speaks with particular pleasure of participating in fund raising and other alumni affairs.

Another trustee, also an alumnus, is a financial consultant whose work brings him into close association with famous personalities in show business. His office is located in a ten-story building that bears his name.

The chairman of the Buildings and Grounds Committee, class of '37, is retired from a senior managerial position and is now a consultant. His activities for his committee are a time-consuming labor of love.

The chairman of the Development Committee, now in his early fifties, has a Ph.D. in one of the sciences. An inventor and successful entrepreneur, he has sold his business and now maintains an office in his home. He is an alumnus.

Longfellow College

Longfellow College is located in a region rich in literary interest. Freshman admission is competitive, with median SAT scores in the mid 500s and acceptance offered to just over half of the applicants. Thirty percent of the students come from within the state, and most of the remainder come from contiguous states. Although Longfellow describes itself as a liberal arts college, one-fourth of its students are majors in the department of economics and business administration. Forty percent of the students pursue graduate or professional studies.

The chairman of the board is chief counsel of a corporation in the Fortune 500, and he says that in pursuing his trustee activities, "my model is the corporate board and its chairman." An alumnus, he has been on the board for seven years, three of them as chairman.

A younger trustee, class of '62, has just resigned as chief executive of a nonprofit organization that promotes environmental causes. Not an active alumnus until he was asked a few years ago to assist in fund raising because he has "contacts" in the philanthropic world, he has been a trustee for three years.

The secretary of the board is an alumna with a history of active participation in college affairs. A national leader and board member in her church, she has been a member of the Longfellow board for seven years.

The president of the college is Simon J. Crawford. Now in his fifties, he received his undergraduate education at a small liberal arts college not far from Longfellow and his Ph.D. from an Ivy League university. After serving elsewhere in several administrative posts, he

came to Longfellow, his first presidency, three years ago. He feels
that institutional planning is one of his managerial strengths.

Melville College

Melville College occupies a campus of several hundred acres that
gives it a rural feel despite its citified environs. Approached by a
winding roadway, its red brick classrooms and dormitories are hidden
from the surrounding neighborhoods. The college draws nearly
three-quarters of its students from in-state and about half of those
who apply are accepted. Median SAT scores fall in the mid 500s.
About one-third of the graduates pursue further study.

The president of the college, now in his sixth year in office, was
schooled at an elite West Coast university and came to Melville from
an administrative position in a state university system. He is said to
have an independent income.

The chairman of the Development Committee is an experienced
community volunteer who has been chairman of a major civic board.
An alumna of the college who graduated twenty years ago, she has
thought carefully about the role of volunteer boards.

The chairman of the Audit Committee is the husband of an alumna.
He is a lawyer who clerked at the Supreme Court following his Ivy
League schooling and was asked to join the Melville board when he
was thirty-two. He is now forty and a partner in a metropolitan law
firm.

A young trustee elected to the board by her classmates at the end
of her senior year is now completing her second year on the board.
Already on a "fast track" as an executive in the technical division of
a large computer manufacturer, she says that as a student she "never
realized how much was going on" behind the scenes in the administration and board room.

The chairman of the board is chief operating officer of a company
in the Fortune 500. Long a friend of the college, he is sympathetic
to the limitations which shared governance places upon the powers
of the college presidency.

Poe College

The campus of Poe College is dotted with large evergreens, and
the major academic buildings, faced in buff brick and brownstone,
line either side of the main street in a small town. Median SAT scores
for entering freshmen fall in the mid 500s, and 70 percent of those
who enroll graduate. Admission is competitive, with 60 percent of

those who apply being accepted. About one-half of the graduates pursue further study.

The president of the college, Dr. Bert Fallows, is in the fifth year of this, his first, presidency. A social scientist who tries to remain current in his field, Dr. Fallows is admired among Poe trustees as an energetic, ambitious, and knowledgeable scholar-administrator.

The chairman of the board is the president and an important shareholder of an industrial company located not far from the campus. Although himself Ivy-educated, the chairman has nonetheless taken a special interest in the college, of which his family has long been a patron.

Another family with a tradition of patronage of the college is represented on the board by a successful executive, now retired. For many years a loyal and active alumnus, this trustee describes himself as "deeply interested in education" and has been a member of the board for over fifteen years.

A third board member, also retired, attended the college on scholarship and says, "I owe Poe College something." On the board for five years, he is presently an independent consultant and is pleased to feel that he now has more time to give to college affairs than in the past, "when my time was not my own."

The youngest member of the board, class of '70, is a lawyer in practice in a city twenty miles from campus. Active as an undergraduate, he had occasions then to make presentations to the board but was surprised to be appointed a member at age twenty-five, shortly after his graduation from law school. He expects to serve on the Poe board for forty years.

Salinger College

Salinger College is located in a town that is the distant suburb of an industrial city. The college accepts three out of every four applicants, and 70 percent of its students come from within the state. Median SAT scores fall in the mid 500s, and about half of the graduates pursue further study.

The president of Salinger is a graduate of a small, elite men's college and at fifty-five has been in office for a decade. Because the college's enrollment has so far remained stable, he has become weary of the "prophets of doom and gloom who have been telling us for years" to expect enrollment declines; still, he wonders, "When is our turn going to come?"

The chairman of the board is perhaps sixty-five and a federal judge. A graduate of Salinger, he calls the tradition that the college has a good academic reputation "an accident of history":

> One hundred years ago there weren't many schools, and Salinger turned out a lot of ministers and lawyers. . . . Institutions have reputations built on years and years of impressions, just like people.

A trustee in her late forties is a community volunteer who has been on the board for five years. She says "all alumni are seeing a different campus" now that the fraternities are coed and have moved out of their individual houses into a dormitory-like complex.

The chairman of the Development Committee is a lawyer-lobbyist for an international energy company and is a second generation Salinger graduate. Voluble and visibly enthusiastic about the college, he is pleased to have recruited the son of his company's president as a student.

The head of a statewide social service agency has been on the board for over twenty years and once lived near the campus. He finds that the issues of student rights at Salinger are not too much different from the issues he recalls from his own days as a student there, and he keeps "waiting to hear a new heresy."

Thoreau College

Perched on a hill overlooking what was once a rural crossroads, Thoreau College is surrounded by flourishing suburbia. Freshman admission is competitive, with median SAT scores falling in the mid 500s and just over half of the applicants admitted. Nearly two-thirds of the students are from within the state; 70 percent go on for further study.

The president of the college, Dr. Albert Albans, is a graduate of Thoreau and served the college both as a faculty member and an administrator before becoming president four years ago. Literate and articulate in manner, he draws familiarly on Western literature on the occasions when he makes formal presentations to the board or other campus constituencies.

One of the three women on the board is an alumna who graduated in the early fifties and is professionally associated with an art museum in the large city near the college. Frequently on campus, she is particularly interested in student affairs and the budget.

Another trustee, now in his second term, is a small city lawyer with a keen eye for human foibles and a skepticism about the value of a board that does not ask hard questions. A member of the class of '37, he has long been active in alumni affairs.

A former private university president was appointed to the board over ten years ago as a distinguished outside educator. He now chairs the Academic Affairs Committee.

The chairman of the board, now an emeritus trustee at the Ivy League university of which he is a graduate, is said to be very wealthy. He accepted the board chairmanship reluctantly two years ago and says he would have preferred to see the board headed by an alumnus.

Twain College

With a campus famous for its gothic architecture, Twain College is located in a prosperous rural town. Less than one-third of applicants are admitted, and median SAT scores for entering freshmen exceed 575. Eighty percent of its graduates go on for further study.

The president of Twain, himself an alumnus, came to the presidency a year and a half ago from a senior academic post at a private university. Of the college, he has said: "Privilege is here, especially in the form of immense freedom for learning, and surely [all of us associated with Twain] must share responsibility for making the best of the opportunity."

The chairman of the board is a senior executive officer of a Fortune 500 company that employs thousands of people worldwide. An alumnus of about fifty, he says that Twain is an "institution that deserves the best"—from its board, its faculty, and all of its constituencies.

A younger trustee, who graduated from the college in the early 1960s, has been on the faculty at a prestigious university and is presently on a tour of duty at the headquarters of a federal social action agency. Now in his second term as a board member, he surmises he was put on the board because of his "youth, race, and academic perspective."

The Development Committee chairman, class of 1950, is a senior partner in a metropolitan law firm. He describes himself as "an active alumnus, known through my alumni activities," and he good-humoredly explains his devotion to the college by saying, "Twain has some ridiculous mystique."

The former chairman of the board has achieved distinction as CEO successively of two major corporations. Now about sixty, he enrolled at Twain from a small country high school and values his undergraduate experience for teaching him that one cannot excel at everything and that any choice in life has its costs.

Notes

Introduction

1. Judgments about institutional selectivity are based on data found in *Barron's Profiles of American Colleges,* 12th ed., vol. 1 (Woodbury, N.Y.: Barron's Educational Series, 1980), pp. x–xviii.

2. For enrollment statistics by higher education segment, see Carnegie Council on Policy Studies in Higher Education, *A Classification of Institutions of Higher Education,* rev. ed. (Berkeley, Calif.: Carnegie Council on Policy Studies in Higher Education, 1976), table 2.

For statistical data on boards according to higher education segment, see Irene L. Gomberg and Frank J. Atelsek, *Composition of College and University Governing Boards* (Washington, D.C.: American Council on Education, Higher Education Panel Reports, No. 35, August 1977), pp. 12–13.

For sources of control of higher education institutions, see John A. Creager, "Development of a Revised Higher Education Panel: A Study of the Taxonomy and Sampling of the Institutional Domain of Higher Education" (Washington, D.C.: American Council on Education, mimeo, n.d., but circa 1976). See also National Center for Educational Statistics, Education Directory, Colleges and Universities, 1978–1979 (Washington, D.C.: Government Printing Office, n.d.), p. xxx.

3. Gomberg and Atelsek, *College and University Governing Boards.*

4. Stephen K. Bailey, personal correspondence, August 13, 1981.

Chapter 1. Governance in the Private Liberal Arts College

1. Frederick Rudolph, *The American College and University: A History* (New York: Vintage Books, 1962), p. 166.

2. Lay governance has not been the tradition in Catholic higher education, where administrators and faculty members have often also served their institution as members of the governing board. Lay representation on Catholic college boards of trustees has increased in recent years.

3. Richard Hofstadter and Wilson Smith, eds., *American Higher Education: A Documentary History* (Chicago: University of Chicago Press, 1961), 1:325.

4. Ibid., p. 348.

5. See, for example, Carnegie Commission on Higher Education, *The*

Governance of Higher Education: Six Priority Problems (New York: McGraw-Hill, 1973), p. 32 and J. Victor Baldridge et al., *Policy Making and Effective Leadership* (San Francisco: Jossey-Bass, 1978), p. 218.

6. Carnegie Commission, *Governance of Higher Education,* p. 36.

7. John W. Nason, *The Future of Trusteeship: The Role and Responsibilities of College and University Governing Boards* (Washington, D.C.: Association of Governing Boards of Universities and Colleges, 1975), n. p.

8. John W. Nason, *The Nature of Trusteeship: The Role and Responsibilities of College and University Boards* (Washington, D.C.: Association of Governing Boards of Universities and Colleges, 1982), p. 16.

9. Nason, *The Nature of Trusteeship,* pp. 18–93. The wording in this paragraph and the one following draws upon the phraseology of chapter subheadings in Nason's chapters 3 and 4.

10. Nason, *The Future of Trusteeship,* p. 19.

11. J. L. Zwingle, *Effective Trusteeship: Some Guidelines for New Trustees and Regents* (Washington, D.C.: Association of Governing Boards of Universities and Colleges, 1975), p. 6.

12. A report on the presidency commissioned by the Association of Governing Boards and directed by Clark Kerr is unusual in its attention to the relationship between the board and the president. See *Presidents Make a Difference: Strengthening Presidential Leadership in Colleges and Universities* (Washington, D.C.: Association of Governing Boards of Universities and Colleges, 1984).

13. Michael D. Cohen and James G. March, *Leadership and Ambiguity: The American College President* (New York: McGraw-Hill, 1974), pp. 81–91 and passim.

Chapter 2. How Boards Diminish the Presidency

1. The choice for a president may not be so straightforward as this trustee's comments seem to imply, as David Riesman observes:

> There are some avant garde colleges where presidents who do *not* take firm and unequivocal positions on contested issues lose credibility. . . . [The president of Twain] may have thought that he was preventing worse fractures on campus which would have cost even more alumni support.

Professor Riesman also notes that "[t]he erosion of credibility in a president who refuses to take unequivocal positions is a slower process than the immediate loss of apparent poise by getting up front" (personal correspondence, February 2, 1982).

2. For an overview of anticipated changes in the 1990s that bear on decision making in the 1980s, see "Planning for the Coming Resurgence in Higher Education," *Change,* September 1984, pp. 37–41.

Chapter 3. How Boards Evaluate the President

1. Even in the absence of a crisis, according to a report of the Association of Governing Boards of Universities and Colleges, there is

> some loss of effectiveness on the way in and on the way out of each presidency—making the average period of high productivity probably no more than 80% of this average seven-year span. On the way in, it takes time to get to know the institution. On the way out, the president (and the board) might wish to hold opportunities to decide open to the successor, or the existing president might not wish to make unpopular decisions for fear they will impede consideration for future positions, or the current president might simply have lost interest.

See *Presidents Make a Difference*, p. ix.

2. Douglas Bauer, "Why Big Business Is Firing the Boss," *New York Times Magazine*, March 8, 1981, p. 24.

3. David Vogel, "America's Management Crisis," *The New Republic*, February 7, 1981, p. 22.

4. "Turnover at the Top: Why Executives Are Losing Their Jobs So Quickly," *Business Week*, December 19, 1983, p. 104.

5. Within higher education, the efficacy of formal assessment is itself being assessed. James L. Fisher, president of the Council for Advancement and Support of Education, and Gary H. Quehl, president of the Council of Independent Colleges, assert that "formal presidential evaluation . . . may be the single greatest barrier to a healthy future for higher education." Because "formal, public assessment undermines the authority, status, and potential effectiveness of the president," they advise trustees to eschew the interviews, questionnaires, and outside consultants normally associated with formal evaluation. Instead, they urge the trustees themselves to do the evaluating "according to the mutual goals established annually by the president and the governing board." See the Fisher and Quehl article, "Presidential Assessment: Obstacle to Leadership," *Change*, May/June 1984, pp. 5–7. Similarly, the Commission on Strengthening Presidential Leadership, sponsored by the Association of Governing Boards of Universities and Colleges, concludes that "although . . . formal reviews have more often done harm than good, we believe that reviews of presidents should be carried out informally and annually." The Commission suggests the end of the second year as a time to decide whether the president's tenure is to be of short- or long-term duration; after seven to ten years, a decision about the next five to ten years "seems wise." See *Presidents Make a Difference*, pp. 56–57.

6. Harry Levinson, *Psychological Man* (Cambridge, Mass.: Levinson Institute, 1976), p. 106.

7. Ibid., p. 67.

8. In 1969 Kingman Brewster, then president of Yale University, suggested that the Yale governing board engage in a "systematic reappraisal and explicit consideration of the president's reappointment at some specified interval." See Kingman Brewster, "The Politics of Academia," *School and Society* 98 (April 1970), p. 214.

Chapter 4. Board and President in Crisis: Case Studies

1. See chapter 3, note 8.

Chapter 5. The Lonely Presidency

1. Michael Maccoby, *The Gamesman* (New York: Bantam Books, 1976), chaps. 5 and 6.

Chapter 6. The Board as a Volunteer Group

1. This discussion of volunteerism has been greatly influenced by the first four chapters of James Q. Wilson's *Political Organizations* (New York: Basic Books, 1973).

2. Cohen and March, *Leadership and Ambiguity*, p. 130.

Chapter 7. The Committee System and Key Trustees

1. The argument against investment in corporations with holdings in South Africa asserts that those companies are part of the systematic exploitation of black citizens imposed by apartheid and condoned by the white-dominated South African government. A counterargument, as David Riesman has pointed out, is that "among other considerations, such as encouraging corporations to follow the Sullivan Principles, to track down alleged complicity can be an endless task, as one college found when it sold everything and started afresh." As Professor Riesman also observes, there has been objection as well to "companies regarded as making evil products," such as Nestlé, whose infant formula used in underdeveloped countries has been a subject of controversy (personal correspondence, February 9, 1982).

2. At no institution in this study is a member of the faculty or student body serving on the governing board. Although the exact number of institutions with faculty or student trustees is unknown, a survey of 1,217 private, four-year institutions with a trustee membership of 31,848 reveals that 0.5 percent come from the faculty and 0.8 percent from the student body. See Gomberg and Atelsek, *College and University Governing Boards*, p. 12.

3. Robert Michels, *Political Parties: A Sociological Study of the Oligarchical Tendencies of Modern Democracy*, trans. Eden and Cedar Paul for the 1915 ed. (New York: Dover Publications, 1959), p. 401.

Chapter 10. Recruitment and Retirement in the Board Room

1. The majority of boards in this study include one or more professional educators, all of whom—with the exception of certain presidents emeriti—

are actively employed by, or retired from, other institutions. For reference to the participation of faculty members and students on the boards of their home institutions, see chapter 7, note 2.

2. The term *alumni trustee* signifies any trustee who was an undergraduate at the college; this usage is different from popular parlance in board rooms where this term refers only to individuals nominated by the alumni association.

3. Gomberg and Atelsek, *College and University Governing Boards*, p. 12.

4. "Efforts to Place Women as Heads of Colleges Gain Momentum," *Chronicle of Higher Education*, April 20, 1981, p. 5. A 1983 survey of 2,800 institutions by the American Council on Education found that 9 percent were headed by women compared with 5 percent in 1975. Two-thirds of women presidents are in the private sector. See "254 Colleges Reported to Have Woman Presidents," *Chronicle of Higher Education*, April 18, 1984, p. 2.

Chapter 11. Trustee Judgment and the President's Recommendations

1. Outside directors are distinguished from those directors who are also members of a firm's management. The latter are often referred to as *inside directors* and presumably are not only very knowledgeable about the day-to-day operations of the business but also are not in a position to disagree with the recommendations of the chief executive officer.

2. See "Arthur Goldberg on Public Directors," *Business and Society Review*, Spring 1973, p. 37.

3. Harold S. Geneen, "Why Directors Can't Protect the Shareholders," *Fortune*, September 17, 1984, p. 28.

4. It is interesting that Geneen suggests a relation between a corporation's board and the company similar to that between a collegiate governing board and the college; however, Geneen assumes that a corporation's board would continue to be dominated by business people, whereas collegiate boards are composed principally of noneducators. See Geneen, "Why Directors Can't Protect the Shareholders," p. 34.

5. *Norm* is defined as a rule about how people should act, talk, and think in a given situation. See Michael S. Bassis, Richard J. Gelles, and Ann Levine, *Sociology: An Introduction* (New York: Random House, 1980), p. 75.

6. In a study of the historical development of academic governance and management, Baldridge et al. observe in *Policy Making and Effective Leadership*, pp. 235–36:

> At any given time, a single institution may have a dominant pattern of management and governance, but as different circumstances arise in its environment, in the professional responsibilities of its staff, and in its structure, this pattern is likely to be transformed. For instance, many institutions once dominated by strong presidential power have now developed collegial patterns of operation; but in times of financial crisis, these collegial patterns may be superseded by strong presidents. Thus, any given institution may see-saw back and forth between alternative styles of management as personalities change, the financial situation varies, or the environment makes new demands.

In view of these observations, it is interesting that of the colleges in this study whose financial position is weak in comparison to the relative uncertainty of the economic environment, none has a president described as strong or forceful by members of the board.

Chapter 12. Model I: The Ratifying Board

1. For a concise history of patterns of governance in higher education, see "Special Study: Historical Developments, 1636–1970," in Baldridge et al., *Policy Making and Effective Leadership*, pp. 234–75. Generalization about historical patterns of governance and their evolution is difficult because of variations among institutions; however, it appears that presidents often—but not always—dominated both the governing board and the faculty until the latter part of the nineteenth century. Then a series of well-publicized dismissals of faculty members by trustees, and in some instances by presidents, contributed to the rise of faculty power under the aegis of the American Association of University Professors, established in 1915.

2. David Riesman, personal correspondence, February 25, 1982.

Chapter 13. Model II: The Corporate Board

1. This reference is to a suggestion by the president of Yale University that governing boards periodically evaluate the president. See chapter 3, note 8.

Chapter 15. Commentary on the Three Operating Styles

1. A social group's culture can be defined as its "total man-made environment, including all the material and non-material products of group life" that are transmitted through learning. See George A. Theodorson and Achilles G. Theodorson, *A Modern Dictionary of Sociology* (New York: Crowell, 1969). More informally, culture is "the way we do things around here"— quoted in Terrence E. Deal and Allan A. Kennedy, *Corporate Cultures: The Rites and Rituals of Corporate Life* (Reading, Mass.: Addison-Wesley, 1982), p. 4.

2. See, for example, Ronny E. Turner and Charles Edgley, "Sociological Semanticide: On Reification, Tautology, and the Destruction of Language," *Sociological Quarterly* 21 (Autumn 1980), pp. 601–2.

Chapter 16. Policy versus Administration

1. In *Policy Making and Effective Leadership* p. 218, Baldridge et al. observe about this change in board members' perspective:

When the flow of incoming students and money is increasing, boards of trustees concern themselves with policy decisions about the operation of the institution.

When money is tight, they tend to move from policy decisions to operational decisions.

2. Richard M. Hodgetts and Max S. Wortman, Jr., *Administrative Policy: Text and Cases in the Policy Sciences* (New York: Wiley, 1975), p. 4.

3. Bertram M. Gross, *The Managing of Organizations: The Administrative Struggle* (New York: Free Press of Glencoe, 1964), p. 313.

4. Paul H. Appleby, *Policy and Administration* (University: University of Alabama Press, 1949), p. 12.

5. Hodgetts and Wortman, *Administrative Policy*, pp. 5–7.

6. Amitai Etzioni, *A Comparative Analysis of Complex Organizations* (New York: Free Press, 1975), pp. 5–6, 40, 48–49, 208.

Chapter 17. The Impact of the Board upon the College

1. In his study of the development of three first-rank liberal arts colleges, Burton R. Clark concludes that charismatic leaders and individuals of great personal force "are not commonly selected by boards of trustees and faculties to be presidents of colleges . . . because such [individuals] are inappropriate for the stability, continuity, and maintenance of the existing power structure. . . . [Charismatic leaders] seize and demand, rather than follow the rules and respond to others. In normal times they are judged too disruptive." See *The Distinctive College: Antioch, Reed, and Swarthmore* (Chicago: Aldine, 1970), p. 241.

2. For a useful account of the strategic approach to planning in higher education, see George Keller, *Academic Strategy: The Management Revolution in American Higher Education* (Baltimore: Johns Hopkins University Press, 1983).

Chapter 18. Some Implications for Theory and Practice

1. Alexander Brody, *The American State and Higher Education* (Washington, D.C.: American Council on Education, 1935), p. 21.

2. See, for example, Wilson, *Political Organizations*, pp. 227–228.

3. See chapter 7, p. 62.

4. David Riesman, personal correspondence, December 16, 1981.

Appendix I. Methodology

1. National Center for Educational Statistics, *Education Directory*, 1978–1979, p. xxix; Creager, "Development of a Revised Higher Education Panel"; Carnegie Council on Policy Studies in Higher Education, *A Classification of Institutions of Higher Education*, rev. ed.; and Baldridge et al., *Policy Making and Effective Leadership*, pp. 58–61.

2. All the colleges in this study have sectarian roots, except for the most

recently established institution, which was founded in the early part of this century. This is not surprising considering that, of the 182 colleges that achieved permanence before the Civil War, 160 were denominational. See Donald G. Tewksbury, *The Founding of American Colleges and Universities before the Civil War* (1932; repr. n.p.: Archon Books, 1965), pp. 32–54. Two of the colleges in this study, while declaring themselves nonsectarian, nonetheless have several seats on their boards designated for church representatives, but the religious influence is diffuse and informal, and the tone of these boards remains nondenominational.

3. Junius A. Davis and Steve A. Batchelor, *The Effective College and University Board: A Report of a National Survey of Trustees and Presidents* (Research Triangle Park, N.C.: Research Triangle Institute, 1974), appendix A, pp. A3–A4.

4. *Barron's Profiles of American Colleges*, 12th ed., pp. x–xviii.

5. Virginia Ann Fadil and Julianne Still Thrift, *Openings, Closings, Mergers and Accreditation Status of Independent Colleges and Universities, Winter 1970 through Summer 1978* (Washington, D.C.: National Institute of Independent Colleges and Universities, 1978), p. 66.

6. See pp. xx–xxi.

Bibliography

A Classification of Institutions of Higher Education. Rev. ed. Berkeley, Calif: Carnegie Council on Policy Studies in Higher Education, 1976.

Allison, Graham T. *Essence of Decision: Explaining the Cuban Missile Crisis.* Boston: Little, Brown, 1971.

Appleby, Paul H. *Policy and Administration.* University: University of Alabama Press, 1949.

"Arthur Goldberg on Public Directors: A Business and Society Review Interview." *Business and Society Review* (Spring 1973): 35–39.

Astin, Alexander W., and Lee, Calvin B. T. *The Invisible Colleges: A Profile of Small, Private Colleges with Limited Resources.* New York: McGraw-Hill, 1972.

Astin, Alexander W., and Sherrei, Rita A. *Maximizing Leadership Effectiveness.* San Francisco: Jossey-Bass, 1980.

Bailey, Stephen K. "The Peculiar Mixture: Public Norms and Private Space." In *Government Regulation of Higher Education,* ed. Walter C. Hobbs. Cambridge, Mass.: Ballinger Publishing Company, 1978.

Baldridge, J. Victor; Curtis, David V.; Ecker, George; and Riley, Gary L. *Policy Making and Effective Leadership.* San Francisco: Jossey-Bass, 1978.

Barron's Profiles of American Colleges. 12th ed., Vol. 1. Woodbury, N.Y.: Barron's Educational Series, 1980.

Bassis, Michael S.; Gelles, Richard J.; and Levine, Ann. *Sociology: An Introduction.* New York: Random House, 1980.

Bauer, Douglas. "Why Big Business Is Firing the Boss." *New York Times Magazine,* March 8, 1981, 24.

Baum, Edward. "The Appointment, Evaluation, and Termination of Academic Administrators." *AAHE Bulletin* 32 (September 1979): 9.

Berelson, Bernard, and Steiner, Gary A. *Human Behavior: An Inventory of Scientific Findings.* New York: Harcourt Brace & World, 1964.

———. *Human Behavior: Shorter Edition.* New York: Harcourt Brace & World, 1967.

Berry, Jeffrey M. *Lobbying for the People.* Princeton, N.J.: Princeton University Press, 1977.

Boulton, William R. "The Nature and Format of Director Information Flows: An Exploratory Study." D.B.A. thesis, Graduate School of Business Administration, Harvard University, 1977. Available through University Microfilms International, Ann Arbor, Mich.

Breneman, David. "Economic Trends: What Do They Imply for Higher Education? *AAHE Bulletin* 32 (September 1979): 1.

Breneman, David W., and Finn, Chester E., Jr. *Public Policy and Private Higher Education*. Washington, D.C.: Brookings Institution, 1978.

Brewster, Kingman. "The Politics of Academia." *School and Society* 98 (April 1970): 214.

Brody, Alexander. *The American State and Higher Education*. Washington, D.C.: American Council on Education, 1935.

Carnegie Commission on Higher Education. *The Governance of Higher Education: Six Priority Problems*. New York: McGraw-Hill, 1973.

Cartwright, Dorwin, and Zander, Alvin. *Group Dynamics*. New York: Harper & Row, 1968.

Clark, Burton R. *The Distinctive College: Antioch, Reed, and Swarthmore*. Chicago: Aldine, 1970.

Cleary, Robert E. "Trustee-President Authority Relations." *Educational Record* (Spring 1979): 146–58.

Cohen, Michael D., and March, James G. *Leadership and Ambiguity: The American College President*. New York: McGraw-Hill, 1974.

Conklin, Harold C. "Ethnography." In *International Encyclopedia of the Social Sciences*, ed. David L. Sills. New York: MacMillan, 1968.

Cowley, W. H. *Presidents, Professors, and Trustees*. San Francisco: Jossey-Bass, 1980.

Creager, John A. "Development of a Revised Higher Education Panel: A Study of the Taxonomy and Sampling of the Institutional Domain of Higher Education." Washington, D.C.: American Council on Education, n.d., but circa 1976. Mimeo.

Davis, Junius A., and Batchelor, Steve A. *The Effective College and University Board: A Report of a National Survey of Trustees and Presidents*. Research Triangle Park, N.C.: Research Triangle Institute, 1974.

Deal, Terrance E., and Kennedy, Allan A. *Corporate Cultures: The Rites and Rituals of Corporate Life*. Reading, Mass.: Addison-Wesley, 1982.

Dexter, Lewis Anthony. *Elite and Specialized Interviewing*. Evanston, Ill.: Northwestern University Press, 1970.

Dominguez, J. T. "To Reign or to Rule: A Choice for University Boards of Trustees." *Connecticut Law Review* 3 (1971): 375–88.

"Efforts to Place Women as Heads of Colleges Gain Momentum." *Chronicle of Higher Education*, April 20, 1981, 5.

Etzioni, Amitai. *A Comparative Analysis of Complex Organizations*. New York: Free Press, 1975.

———. *Complex Organizations: A Sociological Reader*. New York: Holt, Rinehart and Winston, 1966.

———. *Modern Organizations*. Englewood Cliffs, N.J.: Prentice-Hall, 1964.

Fadil, Virginia Ann, and Thrift, Julianne Still. *Openings, Closings, Mergers and Accreditation Status of Independent Colleges and Universities, Winter 1970 through Summer 1978*. Washington, D.C.: National Institute of Independent Colleges and Universities, 1978.

Fisher, James L., and Quehl, Gary H., "Presidential Assessment: Obstacle to Leadership." *Change* (May/June 1984): 5–7.

Friedrich, Carl J., ed. *The Public Interest*. New York: Atherton Press, 1966.

"Functions of Boards of Trustees in Higher Education." Philadelphia: Commission on Higher Education, Middle States Association of Colleges and Schools. June 1978. Mimeo.

Galbraith, John Kenneth. "How Can the University Protect Itself?" *College Management* 1 (September 1967): 34.

Geneen, Harold S. "Why Directors Can't Protect the Shareholders." *Fortune*, September 17, 1984, 28–32.

Gerth, H. H., and Mills, C. Wright. *From Max Weber: Essays in Sociology*. New York: Oxford University Press, 1958.

Glazer, Nathan. "Regulating Business and the Universities: One Problem or Two?" *The Public Interest* 56 (Summer 1979): 43–65.

Gomberg, Irene L., and Atelsek, Frank J. *Composition of College and University Governing Boards*. Washington, D.C.: American Council on Education, Higher Education Panel Reports, No. 35, August 1977.

Gouldner, Alvin W., ed. *Studies in Leadership: Leadership and Democratic Action*. New York: Russell and Russell, 1965.

Grant, W. Vance, and Lind, C. George. *Digest of Education Statistics 1977–1978*. Washington, D.C.: Government Printing Office, 1978.

Gross, Bertram M. *The Managing of Organizations: The Administrative Struggle*. 2 vols. New York: Free Press of Glencoe, 1964.

Gwyn, W. B. *The Meaning of the Separation of Powers*. Tulane Studies in Political Science IX. New Orleans: Tulane University, 1965.

Haller, Max. "Marriage, Women, and Social Stratification: A Theoretical Critique." *American Journal of Sociology* (January 1981): 766–95.

Hare, A. Paul. *Handbook of Small Group Research*. New York: Free Press, 1976.

Hartnett, Rodney T. "College and University Trustees: Their Backgrounds, Roles, and Educational Attitudes." In *Academic Governance*, ed. J. Victor Baldridge. Berkeley, Calif.: McCatchan, 1971.

Healy, Rose M., and Peterson, Vance T. "Trustee and College Failure: A Study of the Role of the Board in Four Small College Terminations." Washington, D.C.: Association of Governing Boards of Universities and Colleges, October 1976. Xeroxed.

Henderson, Algo D. "The Role of the Governing Board." In *Academic Governance*, ed. J. Victor Baldridge. Berkeley, Calif.: McCatchan, 1971.

Hendrickson, Robert M., and Mangum, Robert Scott. *Governing Board and Administrator Liability*. Higher Education Research Report No. 9. Washington, D.C.: American Association of Higher Education, 1977.

Hobbs, Walter C. "The Theory of Government Regulation." In *Government Regulation of Higher Education*, ed. Walter C. Hobbs. Cambridge, Mass.: Ballinger, 1978.

Hodgetts, Richard M., and Wortman, Max S., Jr. *Administrative Policy: Text and Cases in the Policy Sciences*. New York: Wiley, 1975.

Hofstadter, Richard, and Smith, Wilson, eds. *American Higher Education: A Documentary History.* Vol. I. Chicago: University of Chicago Press, 1961.

Howe, Harold II. "What Future for the Private College?" *Change* (May/June 1979): 28.

Hull, W. Frank, and Shapiro, Allen H. *The University Trustee in Law and Practice.* University of Toledo: Center for the Study of Higher Education, 1973.

Ingram, Richard T., ed. *Handbook of College and University Trusteeship.* San Francisco: Jossey-Bass, 1980.

———. "Trustees—Power and Sanity in the 1980s." *Educational Record* 61 (Winter 1980): 24–29.

Jencks, Christopher, and Riesman, David. *The Academic Revolution.* New York: Doubleday, 1968.

Kanter, Rosabeth Moss. *Men and Women of the Corporation.* New York: Basic Books, 1977.

Kaplan, William A. *The Law of Higher Education: Legal Implications of Administrative Decision Making.* San Francisco: Jossey-Bass, 1979.

Kauffman, Joseph F. *At the Pleasure of the Board: The Service of the College and University President.* Washington, D.C.: American Council on Education, 1980.

Keller, George. *Academic Strategy: The Management Revolution in American Higher Education.* Baltimore: Johns Hopkins University Press, 1983.

Levinson, Harry. *Psychological Man.* Cambridge, Mass.: Levinson Institute, 1976.

Levy, Leslie. "Reforming Board Reform." *Harvard Business Review* (January-February 1981): 166–72.

Lindblom, Charles E. "The Science of Muddling Through." In *Readings on Modern Organizations,* ed. Amitai Etzioni. Englewood Cliffs, N.J.: Prentice-Hall, 1969.

Lowi, Theodore. *The End of Liberalism: Ideology, Policy, and the Crisis of Public Authority.* New York: Norton, 1969.

Maccoby, Michael. *The Gamesman.* New York: Bantam Books, 1976.

Mace, Myles L. *Directors: Myth and Reality.* Boston: Harvard Graduate School of Business Administration, 1971.

———. "Standards of Care for Trustees." *Harvard Business Review* (January-February 1976): 14.

Martin, Warren Bryan. *A College of Character: Renewing the Purpose and Content of College Education.* San Francisco: Jossey-Bass, 1982.

Martorana, S. V. *College Boards of Trustees.* Washington, D.C.: Center for Applied Research in Education, 1963.

Michels, Robert. *Political Parties: A Sociological Study of the Oligarchical Tendencies of Modern Democracy.* Trans. Eden and Cedar Paul for the 1915 ed. New York: Dover Publications, 1959.

Millett, John D. *Strengthening Community in Higher Education.* New York: Academy for Educational Development, 1974.

Minter, W. John, and Bowen, Howard R. *Independent Higher Education: Fourth*

Annual Report on Financial and Educational Trends in the Independent Sector of Higher Education. Washington, D.C.: National Association of Independent Colleges and Universities, 1978.

Myrdal, Gunnar. *Value in Social Theory: A Selection of Essays on Methodology.* New York: Harper & Brothers, 1958.

Nason, John W. *Presidential Assessment: A Challenge to College and University Leadership.* Washington, D.C.: Association of Governing Boards of Universities and Colleges, 1980.

————. *Presidential Search: A Guide to the Process of Selecting and Appointing College and University Presidents.* Washington, D.C.: Association of Governing Boards of Universities and Colleges, 1979.

————. *The Future of Trusteeship: The Role and Responsibilities of College and University Governing Boards.* Washington, D.C.: Association of Governing Boards of Universities and Colleges, 1975.

————. *The Nature of Trusteeship: The Role and Responsibilities of College and University Boards.* Washington, D.C.: Association of Governing Boards of Universities and Colleges, 1982.

National Center for Education Statistics. *Education Directory, Colleges and Universities, 1978–1979.* Washington, D.C.: Government Printing Office, n.d.

Newman, Frank. "Trustee Accountability and National Policy." *AGB Reports* 16 (October 1973): n. p.

Paltridge, James G.; Hurst, Julie; and Morgan, Anthony. *Boards of Trustees: Their Decision Patterns.* Berkeley, Calif.: Center for Research and Development in Higher Education, University of California, 1973.

Perkins, James A., ed. *The University as an Organization.* New York: McGraw-Hill, 1973.

Pool, Ithiel de Sola. *Contemporary Political Science: Toward Empirical Theory.* New York: McGraw-Hill, 1967.

Porth, William C. "Personal Liability of Trustees of Educational Institutions." *Journal of College and University Law* (Winter 1974–75): 143–56.

Presidents Make a Difference: Strengthening Leadership in Colleges and Universities. Washington, D.C.: Association of Governing Boards of Universities and Colleges, 1984.

Rauh, Morton A. *The Trusteeship of Colleges and Universities.* New York: McGraw-Hill. 1969.

Riesman, David. *Abundance for What: And Other Essays.* Garden City, N.Y.: Doubleday, 1964.

Riesman, David, and McLaughlin, Judith. "A Primer on the Use of Consultants in Presidential Recruitment." *Change* (September 1984): 12.

Riley, Gary L., and Baldridge, J. Victor. *Governing Academic Organizations: New Problems, New Perspectives.* Berkeley, Calif.: McCatchan, 1977.

Rudolph, Frederick. *The American College and University: A History.* New York: Vintage Books, 1962.

————. Review of *Presidents, Professors, and Trustees* by W. H. Cowley. *Journal of Higher Education* 52 (May-June 1981): 321–23.

Schenkel, Walter. "Who Has Been in Power?" In *Power and Authority* ed. Harold L. Hodgkinson and L. Richard Meeth. San Francisco: Jossey-Bass, 1971.

Schubert, Glendon. *The Public Interest.* New York: Free Press of Glencoe, 1960.

Sills, David L. "Voluntary Associations: Sociological Aspects." In *International Encyclopedia of the Social Sciences,* ed. David L. Sills. New York: Macmillan, 1968.

Slonim, Morris James. *Sampling.* New York: Simon & Schuster, 1960.

Smith, Constance, and Freedman, Anne. *Voluntary Associations: Perspectives on the Literature.* Cambridge: Harvard University Press, 1972.

Smith, Hoke L. "Planning for the Coming Resurgence in Higher Education." *Change* (September 1984): 37.

Tewksbury, Donald G. *The Founding of American Colleges and Universities before the Civil War.* 1932; repr. n.p.: Archon Books, 1965.

Theodorson, George A., and Theodorson, Achilles G. *A Modern Dictionary of Sociology.* New York: Crowell, 1969.

Thwing, Charles F. *A History of Higher Education in America.* New York: D. Appleton and Company, 1906.

Tocqueville, Alexis de. *Democracy in America.* Abridged. New York: Washington Square Press, 1964.

Tucker, Allan, and Mautz, Robert B. "Presidential Evaluation: An Academic Circus." *Educational Record* (Summer 1979): 253–60.

Turner, Ronny E., and Edgley, Charles. "Sociological Semanticide: On Reification, Tautology, and the Destruction of Language." *Sociological Quarterly* 21 (Autumn 1980): 595–605.

"Turnover at the Top: Why Executives Are Losing Their Jobs So Quickly." *Business Week,* December 19, 1983, 104 ff.

"254 Colleges Reported to Have Woman Presidents." *Chronicle of Higher Education,* April 18, 1984, p. 2.

"Uneasy Men at the Top." *Newsweek,* July 7, 1980, 54.

Veblen, Thorstein. *The Higher Learning in America: A Memorandum on the Conduct of Universities by Businessmen.* New York: Sagamore Press, 1957.

Vesey, Laurence R. *The Emergence of the American University.* Chicago: University of Chicago Press, 1965.

Vogel, David. "America's Management Crisis." *The New Republic,* February 7, 1981, 22.

Warwick, Donald P. *A Theory of Public Bureaucracy.* Cambridge, Mass.: Harvard University Press, 1975.

Wilson, James Q. *Political Organizations.* New York: Basic Books, 1973.

Zwingle, J. L. *Effective Trusteeship: Some Guidelines for New Trustees and Regents.* Washington, D.C.: Association of Governing Boards of Universities and Colleges, 1975.

———. "Governing Boards." In *Handbook of College and University Administration,* ed. Asa S. Knowles. New York: McGraw-Hill, 1970.

Index

THE JOHNS HOPKINS UNIVERSITY PRESS

TRUSTEESHIP IN THE PRIVATE COLLEGE

This book was composed in Baskerville text and display type by Monotype Composition Company. It was printed on 50-lb. Glatfelter Offset and bound in Kivar 5 by Thomson-Shore, Inc.